IMAGES of America

DOUGLASTON–LITTLE NECK

A Beautiful Situation. The town of Douglaston sits upon a peninsula overlooking Little Neck Bay. The attractive fin-shaped wedge of land featured more than 1,000 lots for sale at the turn of the 20th century after the Rickert-Finlay Realty Company purchased the area from the family of William Proctor Douglas, son of the town's founder George Douglas. Located 13.9 miles from Manhattan's Pennsylvania Station, the town is shown here during its glorious early stage of development from farmland and private estates to city suburb. (Douglaston and Little Neck Historical Society.)

On the Cover: Trying to Beat the Rush Hour. The more things change, the more they remain the same. Stuck in westbound rush hour traffic on Northern Boulevard just east of Little Neck Parkway, this smiling motorist would be amused to know that he is on the cover of a local history book published more than 93 years after a photographer from the Queens Topographical Bureau snapped this photograph on May 22, 1927. (NYC Municipal Archives.)

IMAGES
of America

DOUGLASTON–LITTLE NECK

Jason D. Antos
Foreword by Donna Gentle Spirit Barron

ARCADIA
PUBLISHING

ISBN 978-1-4671-0545-3

Published by Arcadia Publishing
Charleston, South Carolina

Printed in the United States of America

Library of Congress Control Number: 2020934345

For all general information, please contact Arcadia Publishing:
Telephone 843-853-2070
Fax 843-853-0044
E-mail sales@arcadiapublishing.com
For customer service and orders:
Toll-Free 1-888-313-2665

Visit us on the Internet at www.arcadiapublishing.com

For my father

Contents

Foreword

My name is Donna Gentle Spirit Barron. I am a Matinecock Indian of Little Neck, New York. I have been the family historian and genealogist for my people for the past 21 years. I first met Jason in 2010; he was showing and lecturing about a documentary that my son made about the Matinecock Indians. After the lecture, Jason so kindly took the time out to meet and talk with my family and me. I got the chance to thank him. His lecture helped give the Matinecock a voice, which was lost when their cemetery was moved to widen a road back in 1931.

The Matinecock history became nearly extinct in Little Neck and Douglaston. But with Jason's help, we gave our ancestors a voice once again! Not only did this true historian lecture about our history, but he also helped keep it alive. Jason had a huge part in a street dedication for the Matinecock in 2015. Because of his love of history and just the wonderful person that he is, the Matinecock now and forever more will be remembered with Matinecock Way.

Since 1636, my family has resided on the same homestead property in Little Neck, New York. It was once a nine-acre property with three homes and a burial ground.

My Matinecock family members were hardworking with a love for their culture and heritage. They were born shell fishermen and clammers. Their lives were spent upon the bay.

By 1931, it all changed. My great-uncle James Wild Pigeon Waters went to court to fight against the City of New York for the removal of the burial ground on the corner of Little Neck Parkway and Northern Boulevard. For the widening of Northern Boulevard, Chief Wild Pigeon lost his life and the fight. Our family had no voice. Not only did they remove the bodies, but they also had museum scientists and archeologists comb through the graves for Indian artifacts. Today, we, the Matinecock family of Little Neck and Douglaston, are happy and thankful for the restoration of our history and plan to keep it alive.

I hope that you will enjoy Jason's new book as much I did. Discovering and learning about such an interesting past leads to a beautiful present day.

—Donna Gentle Spirit Barron
Little Neck, New York, 2020

Acknowledgments

No book is the product of just the author alone. I wish to thank my friends and colleagues who supported me and have helped bring this book, my seventh, to fruition. My thanks go to the board of directors and staff of the Queens Historical Society at Kingsland Homestead and, especially, former board president Patricia Sherwood. To Erik Huber and the staff of the Archives at Queens Borough Public Library (formerly the Long Island Division), I thank them for their tireless assistance in researching and helping to photocopy vital historical materials. To Donna Barron and her entire family, the Matinecock peoples, and also Chief Harry Wallace of the Unkechaug Indian Nation, I am truly blessed by your friendship. Special thanks go to the Douglaston and Little Neck Historical Society and Mike Gannon for his invaluable suggestions and editorial assistance with this project. A big thank-you is given to Arlene Abdalian for her assistance in helping this project get off the ground and also to Arcadia Publishing and Caitrin Cunningham. And of course, I am grateful for my family and friends who have supported my work in preserving the amazing and remarkable history of Queens County for the past 15 years. All images in this book, unless otherwise noted, are from the author's collection, and all modern images were taken by the author.

Introduction

Douglaston . . . is on high ground with a splendid outlook.

—Edward J. Rickert interview,
Architecture and Building, May 1914 issue

The village of Douglaston is situated upon a peninsula overlooking Little Neck Bay. Physically part of Long Island's north shore, the fin-shaped peninsula was created about 21,000 years ago (roughly 19,000 BC) when the island separated from what is today the state of Connecticut. Part of a massive glaciation of ice known as the Wisconsin Glacier, the land upon which Douglaston and Little Neck today sit was created after the sheet of ice separated and moved south, creating the Long Island Sound in between Connecticut and Long Island. As the ice melted, the northern part of the glacial moraine was left rocky and hilly with sizable strips of land separated by small bays called "necks."

These land formations resulted from the trauma caused by the terrain tearing away from the larger landmass. All of this occurred during a period spanning thousands of years. As one travels south along Queens and Long Island, the land noticeably becomes flatter, featuring meadows, swamps, and plains. As the ice melted, the low-lying swampy areas were created in the wake of the waters flowing downward, creating what is known as an outwash plain. The peninsula was covered with trees to the north and meadows to the south. It was upon this beautiful pristine landscaped that the Native Americans lived in longhouses and fished in Little Neck Bay, bountiful with fish and clams.

The first Native Americans appeared on Long Island approximately 2,000 years ago. They were the Lenni-Lenape and spoke Algonquin. These first peoples referred to the area as Matinecock, or "Place of the Hill Country" or "The Hunting Place." They made up one of the largest tribes on Long Island, and their settlement stretched from Newtown Creek in western Queens all the way to the Nissequoque River in Smithtown, Long Island, which measures a distance of almost 50 miles.

At the time of the arrival of the first Europeans, there were approximately 6,500 Native Americans living on Long Island. The Algonquin used a form of currency called wampum, which was made of clamshells. Long Island was so abundant with these shells that the natives called the island Pomonok, or "Land of Tribute." There were many restrictions on the Native Americans and their dealings with Europeans, both Dutch and English.

The area has been known by other names in the past four centuries. It was originally called Little Madnan's Neck, a corruption of the Lenni-Lenape word Men-haden-ock, meaning "Place of Fish." The area was even briefly called Cornbury in the 17th century. Little Neck Bay was known as Matthew Garretson's Bay, and in 1632, a group of Dutch colonialists, led by Garretson, settled not too far from the area. The first English settlers arrived in Queens in May 1640. The county of Queens was known during the early days of the colonial British era as the North Riding of Yorkshire.

It was the Dutch and the West India Trading Company that claimed the northeastern part of America and named it New Netherland in 1624. The main seat of power was New Amsterdam, today's Manhattan Island. It was the third director general of New Netherland, Peter Minuit, who purchased Manhattan Island from Native Americans on May 24, 1626, for 60 Dutch guilders, or $1,100 in today's money.

It was Petrus Stuyvesant, the seventh and final director general of the territory, who, after 17 years of rule, surrendered the colony to England in 1664 after British naval ships surrounded the city on orders of King Charles II. It was rechristened New York in honor of the Duke of York, later King James II of England. Although no longer in control, the Dutch were allowed to live their lives as before with no loss of liberties or land. In 1665, Richard Nicholls was appointed governor of New York. In remapping the territory, Governor Nicholls organized New York into shires and ridings based on the old English model of city planning. In 1683, the area was reorganized again into counties. Queens was named in honor Queen Catherine of Braganza, wife of King Charles II. The British colonial government even recognized wampum as the official currency of the indigenous people in 1674 and passed a law stating that six white wampum or three black wampum would be equal to a penny, or stiver, as it was called then.

And there was of course the matter of land ownership and who shall reside where. In the fall of 1675, Little Neck resident Thomas Hicks wanted to take control of the land comprising all of Little Neck, then known as Cornbury. Hicks hoped to obtain a full land claim, but it was denied partially on the grounds that the local government could not decide whether or not Little Neck was situated in the township of Flushing or the town of North Hempstead, which, centuries later, succeeded from Queens and became part of today's Nassau County, Long Island.

It was 20 years earlier, in 1656, when the area was under Dutch rule, that Hicks led a group of men to push the remaining Matinecock off their land. Historical records confirm that a final battle took place in the village center, which is today the intersection of Northern Boulevard and Marathon Parkway. The effects of this tragic encounter still echo today as one will read later on in this book.

Nonetheless, it was the governor of New York, Edmund Andros, who made the final, yet ill-informed, decision, and it is here that we read of the village of Cornbury for the first time.

Governor Andros declared, "Where I am informed that heretofore in the time of Governor Nicholls, the town called Cornbury or Little Madnan's neck, where Captain Thomas Hicks doth reside . . . it is found that part of the land and neck, belonging Thomas Hicks is within the bounds of Hempstead Township . . . Hicks is now Justice of the Peace for town and Riding. The farm and land upon Cornbury belonging to Captain Thomas Hicks shall be deemed and held to be within the bound and limits of Hempstead and no longer of Flushing. Given under my hand this 23rd day of November 1675."

Thomas Hicks, through aggression and violence, retained most of the property consisting of Little Neck for decades. His descendants would continue living in the area for more than 250 years.

In the days before the arrival of Cornelius Van Wyck and Wyant Van Zandt and the Douglas family, the first European settlements appeared on the neighborhood's western outskirts. Nestled in between Bayside to the west and Douglaston and Little Neck to the east is a long corridor of grassy wetland, which locals affectionately called "the Alley." Extending southward from the mouth of Little Neck Bay all the way to the present-day Long Island Expressway, whose construction three quarters of a century ago destroyed the last vestiges of the Alley Pond and the original homesteads of Douglaston and Little Neck, the Alley has been inhabited and visited by everyone from Native Americans to Pres. George Washington and was once a temporary settlement for emancipated slaves. The source of when the unofficial title or nickname of the Alley was first coined has been lost to time. What is virtually the birthplace of northeast Queens, the Alley was first settled in 1637–1638 by Thomas Foster after he received a land grant by the director general of New Netherland, Peter Stuyvesant. Later, in 1691, the Hick's family erected the area's first mill. On ancient maps of the area, it is labeled as Hick's Mill and was located a short distance south of Northern Boulevard on the property currently occupied by the Alley Pond Environmental Center. The Talman family erected mills. More than a century later, James Hedges came to the Alley and built a gristmill in 1752, which he operated along with a descendant of the Foster family. Locals knew the southern terminus of the Alley as Captain Hick's Landing. John Baird erected a woolen mill in the early 19th century. The mill was in operation until 1820, when it was destroyed by fire. The people of the Algonquin Nation lived here at this time in Little Neck, as it was an ideal location situated near both a bay and meadowland from which they derived an abundance of fish and clams and hunted deer.

In 1828, Benjamin Lowerre, creator of the Flushing Hotel in downtown Flushing, built a general store on the old site of the woolen mill. In 1858, Lowerre sold the store to his brother-in-law William C. Buhrman, who expanded it to include a blacksmith. The Buhrman family prospered and built a large homestead that, along with the store, stood until 1936. It became the first official post office for Flushing Township, and mail was delivered here by stagecoach twice a week.

Journalist and historian Henry Collins Brown, founder of the Museum of the City of New York, wrote about the residents of the Alley in his 1936 book of reminisces of old New York, *From Alley Pond to Rockville Center*, and details a visit he paid to Buhrman's general store and made the following observation: "It is one of those stores that contain everything from anchor chains to chewing gum. There are bicycle sundries in the showcase and boneless bacon suspended from the old rafters, but the best thing in the place is a stream of running water. This is led down by a pipe from the side of the hill and acts as a refrigerator for a sort of bar in one corner of the store."

Little Neck also boasts a proud legacy of men who fought in the Revolutionary and Civil Wars. During the American Revolution, a company of soldiers was formed in the village of North Hempstead, the territory comprising of the eastern part of Queens County, which would become part of Nassau County, Long Island, in 1899. The company was called the North Side Company and consisted of 120 men, including the following Little Neck residents: Capt. Philip Valentine, 2nd Lt. Coe Searing, Capt. David Layton, and Sgts. Lewis Cornell and James Doughty. Eight decades later, in the Civil War, more than 30 citizens of Little Neck were drafted and fought bravely. William H. Pudney fought in the Battle of Mobile Bay. The Zion Church is the final resting place for many veterans of the War Between the States. In 1864, the same church donated $25.80 for the construction of the Patriot Orphan Home in Flushing that housed 92 boys and girls who were orphaned because their fathers died in battle and had no one else to care for them.

Maj. Thomas Wickes, a Revolutionary War soldier, originally from Huntington, Long Island, purchased 300 acres at the Douglaston peninsula in 1795 and called his farm Little Neck. The first major landowner after Major Wickes was Cornelius Van Wyck, who, in 1735, built his homestead in what would later become Douglas Manor more than a century later. In 1813, wealthy Manhattan merchant and city alderman Wyant Van Zandt III came to Douglaston, purchasing land from the family of Cornelius Van Wyck. Unlike his predecessors, Van Zandt was deeply involved in trade city politics. He was on the building committee for city hall and was appointed chairman of the committee overseeing the city's water supply. Van Zandt owned a slave named Margaret Pine, who remained in his service until the family moved to the area. In 1814, Van Zandt gave Margaret her freedom. In her freedom papers, Van Zandt wrote, "The bearer, Margaret Pine, is my servant. She has lived with me from her infancy. She's sober, honest, and faithful and has my permission to go to New York, for the purpose of going out to service, and to receive her wages. I further declare that it is my wish, and I am now willing to manumit her according to law. Given under my hand, at Little Neck Farm, this 5th day of September 1814." Pine died at Little Neck on September 30, 1857, at the age of 78.

By 1830, Wyant Van Zandt used his fortune and civic influence to have a toll road built into Little Neck. The causeway would be an extension built by the North Hempstead and Flushing Turnpike Road and Bridge Company. The road proved problematic as it crossed the marshes of the Alley. The road had been built just above the high-tide mark, and when storms would occur, as they do every spring and winter, the turnpike (Northern Boulevard) would be under water. Tolls collected at a tollgate, located at the present-day Alley Pond Environmental Center, were used to pay for road repairs and improvements to the grade, or the road's elevation. That same year, Van Zandt also donated land for the construction of Zion Episcopal Church. In 1848, Jeremiah Lambertson purchased a small farm at the base of the peninsula. Lambertson mapped lots in 1853 for a suburban subdivision he called the Village of Marathon, anticipating the yet-to-be-built railroad, which arrived in the 1860s. He saved a small portion for his estate and lived there until he died in the late 1850s. His family remained until the 1880s. Although the Village of Marathon was developed with lots, the name never caught on, and further development fizzled out. The Van Zandt family sold off their property to George Douglas in 1835. In 1862, the area passed onto his son William P. Douglas, who helped established a train station and officially designated the peninsula as Douglaston, thus separating it from greater Little Neck and generating the existence of two towns from one.

The legacy of Douglaston and Little Neck is a vital story to the epic and awe-inspiring history of New York City. In 1906, the large real estate concern, the Rickert-Finlay Realty Company, owned by brothers Charles and Edward J. Rickert and their partner Charles E. Finlay, purchased the peninsula and called it Douglas Manor in honor of the family who helped the area become well established.

Finlay and the Rickerts, who hailed from the Midwest, came to New York City to make their fortune. And indeed, they did. In 1902, the Rickert-Finlay Realty Company was established, and by 1908, the company, with offices at 45 West Thirty-fourth Street in Manhattan, was advertising itself as "the Largest Developers of Real Estate in Queens Borough."

Rickert-Finlay began improving the area with cement sidewalks and macadam roads, and trees and hedges were planted. The first residents to move into the manor were the Butlers of Flushing.

With the passion and dedication of the Douglaston community and civic organizations, such as the Douglas Manor Association (formed in 1906 and incorporated in 1981) and the Douglaston and Little Neck Historical Society (established 1989), the community of Douglas Manor achieved a victory after a nine-year quest, when the Landmarks Commission of New York City awarded landmark district designation, thus creating the Douglaston Historic District in 1997. The district includes the almost 600 Douglas Manor homes, comprising of various architectural beauty and distinction, as well as the 1.5-mile-long landscaped waterfront overlooking Little Neck Bay. The original street names have also been preserved. Rickert-Finlay and the Douglas family would be pleased to have known that their creation lives on now for future generations, and both Douglaston and Little Neck remain today as some of the most sought after neighborhoods in New York City in which to live, work, and raise a family.

—Jason D. Antos
Whitestone, New York, 2020

One

The Early Days of Douglaston and Little Neck

Objects from the Past. During an archeological dig near Oakland Lake, located a short distance away in neighboring Bayside, on October 29, 1932, scientists discovered remnants from the earliest civilization of Queens and Long Island. Fragments of clay pots and an arrowhead, created by the Native Americans who referred to the area as Matinecock, were found. The same team of archeologists also made similar discoveries at Woodhaven in southern Queens; those artifacts belonged to the Carnarsie, which means "fortified village" in the Lenape language, who occupied southern Queens and Brooklyn. (Ralph S. Solecki Collection, Archives at Queens Borough Public Library.)

Cornelius Van Wyck. The grandson of Dutch immigrants who came to the New World when the territory was a colony of the Dutch West India Company and known as New Amsterdam, Cornelius Van Wyck built his homestead here in the former village of Cornbury, now known as Little Neck (and then Douglaston a century later), in 1735. Pictured here is a descendant, Cornelius Van Wyck Lawrence. Born in 1791, Lawrence was mayor of New York City from 1834 to 1837.

Wyant Van Zandt III. It was in 1813 when Wyant Van Zandt III (1767–1831), a wealthy merchant of dry goods, a vestryman of Manhattan's Trinity Church, and a New York City alderman, came to the future Douglaston peninsula and purchased 120 acres for $25,000 from Thomas Weeks. Van Zandt resided in the city and, like most persons of means, purchased property in the countryside, located outside of the heavily populated Manhattan and Brooklyn areas, in order to escape outbreaks of yellow fever and malaria, which plagued the city during the summer months. He called his homestead Little Neck Farm.

A LEGITIMATE KNICKERBOCKER. On October 31, 1851, the *Brooklyn Daily Eagle* ran a story focusing on Dr. Charles A. Van Zandt, son of Wyant Van Zandt, who was the Democratic nominee for city coroner. The article briefly celebrated the legacy of the Van Zandt family and discussed the purchase of the farm property known as "Little Neck." It called the elder a "gentleman" and one who "held a commanding influence in the affairs" of New York City.

Our Candidate for Coroner.

Dr. Chas. A. Van Zandt, the Democratic nominee for Coroner of this City, is a member of a family that has filled a large space in the public eye, and maintained an honorable rank in society for a century and a half. It has shared largely in the local and political affairs of New York, and at all times has been respected for its devotion to the republican institutions of the country.

Dr. Van Zandt is the son of the late Wynant Van Zandt, who retired from business in the City of New York, in 1812, and purchased the well known property called Little Neck, near to Flushing, on this island, and where the Doctor resided nearly all the early part of his life; and he is generally claimed as a legitimate Long Islander. His father was a gentleman who was in his day and generation regarded as first among the legitimate Knickerbockers, and who at the same time held a commanding influence in the affairs of the City of New York.

VILLAGE OF MARATHON, 1859. In keeping with a popular marketing trend of its day, Douglaston was known originally as Marathon. The origin of the name derives from classical Greek literature and is part of a repeating format in which a multitude of towns in New York state, as well as around the country, were named after characters or places in order to give the neighborhood an air of sophistication and, at times, reflected the founding developer's classical education. Other examples of this trend include towns like Ithaca and Ulysses, New York, and long-distance places like Athens, Georgia, and Phoenix, Arizona.

The Cornelius Van Wyck House. Built in 1735 by Van Wyck, this Dutch Colonial house is one of the last remaining in New York City. The home was expanded by his son Stephen, a delegate to the Continental Congress, during a 30-plus-year period until 1770. Wyant Van Zandt purchased the home in 1813. The notable architectural features of the house include its saltbox roof, oak beams, and wooden shingles. It was designated a New York City landmark in 1966 and placed in the National Register of Historic Places in 1983. (Bob Stonehill collection.)

Douglas Manor Inn. Six years after his arrival to what locals called "the Point," Wyant Van Zandt moved from the Conrelius Van Wyck property and built this stately manor house in 1819 for use as a family homestead. After Van Zandt's death, his heirs began selling off his vast real estate holdings to the Douglas family. With a frontage of 1,275 feet, the estate occupied an entire block facing Little Neck Bay. Featuring an observation cupola on its roof, the estate was purchased in 1835 by George Douglas and was later owned by his son William P. Douglas, who took over the property at the age of 20. The crown jewel of Douglas Manor, the Van Zandt–Douglas mansion, was transformed into a small hotel with a bar and dining room in 1906.

Two

Down in This Happy Valley

The Alley. The full span of the meadows, seen from the southern end of the Alley, is shown here looking north to Little Neck Bay. This photograph from 1920 shows the area almost as it was when the Hicks family arrived in the mid-1600s. Far off in the distance to the northeast (upper right) is Douglaston. Journalist and historian Henry Collins Brown wrote about the Alley in his 1936 book *From Alley Pond to Rockville Center* and stated, "The fact that they are in Greater New York does not seem to bother them much down in this happy valley; at least it hasn't changed their mode of life apparently."

WETLANDS. The pristine wetlands of the Alley are today a protected environmental preserve. In this 1917 image, taken by Great Neck photographer Boris Stackliff, the farming community of Little Neck can be seen in its early days when it was a small sleepy village tucked away behind the Alley at the easternmost terminus of New York City. (Borough President of Queens Collection, Archives at Queens Borough Public Library.)

THE FOSTER HOMESTEAD. Thomas Foster built this one-story house of stone and shingles on his more than 600 acres of land in 1637. Located near the Alley Pond, the house was east of the present-day intersection of the Long Island Expressway and Cross Island Parkway. Seven generations of Fosters would occupy this site. The home had wooden shutters and an upper level, which served as an attic. Legend has it that the attic was built as a hiding place in case of attacks from local Indian tribes. A rope ladder was used to access the room. Once the family was inside, the ladder could be pulled up through a trap door, which was then shut tight to keep everyone safe.

The Foster House in Later Years. In 1663, Thomas Foster expanded the house and built a small stone storage shed next to the remolded home, which eliminated the safe room (for no attacks from Native Americans ever came), and thus, a second story, featuring living quarters, was established. The homestead site, now buried and long forgotten under heavily traveled expressways, boasted two interesting events during the American Revolution. The first was the visit of a British sea captain who presented Foster with a cutting from a pear tree. From this cutting, the first Bartlett pears in this country were grown. The second, during the height of the fighting, enemy troops, allegedly Hessians, ransacked the Foster homestead and hung Thomas Foster from a tree. He was rescued but was scarred emotionally for the remainder of his days.

The Alley Gristmill. Hundreds of years ago, gristmills were an essential part of the community as colonists used them to grind grain crops into food to be consumed by both people and animals. They were also gathering places where locals would come and talk about the news of the day, inquire about each other's families, and trade gossip. Located just south of Northern Boulevard, the mill was operated by a small stream fed from the bay into Alley Creek, which turned the turbine and rotated the heavy mill stones that mashed wheat into grain. Originally operated by the Hicks family, the Talman family operated the mill in the 1700s and then James Hedges in 1752. Pictured here in 1926 are the ruins of the abandoned mill after it was destroyed by fire.

Buhrman's Alley. The Alley's most prosperous resident was William Buhrman, a German immigrant who painted houses and signs. First established by Flushing innkeeper Benjamin Lowerre in 1828, the general store was then taken over by Buhrman, who was Lowerre's son-in-law. For almost a century, the Buhrman general store was one of the most patronized establishments in the area. The property surrounded the Alley Pond and featured several structures. The area became known during this time as "Buhrman's Alley."

The Buhrman Homestead. The Buhrman property featured a small gristmill, several storage houses, a barn, post office, general store, and the four-story mansion on the left.

THE LOWERRE/BUHRMAN GENERAL STORE. Before Douglas Manor was the centerpiece of the area, the most visited establishment in Little Neck and Douglaston was Buhrman's general store. Here, residents could buy kerosene oil for lamps, sugar and flour, calico for dresses, pants, shoes, butter, crackers and molasses, bacon, and fresh eggs. According to surviving records from the late 1890s, a pound of sugar sold for 6¢, butter for 25¢, a pound sack of flour went for 75¢, and coffee and tea went for 15¢ a pound. In this haunting photograph showing the general store in its final years, Queens Borough president Maurice M. Connolly can be seen posing on the right.

INSIDE THE GENERAL STORE. Illustrated by William Jessie Lynch, the interior of the general store is shown here as it appeared in 1902. Journalist and historian Henry Collins Brown wrote about the general store in his 1936 memoir *From Alley Pond to Rockville Center*. "The old store, presumably the polling place of that election district of the city, is where prominent personages of the neighborhood congregate and tell fishing and shooting stories, gossip and talk politics, seated on boxes and barrels around the white bodied stove, for the sake of which they chew tobacco," Brown reminisced.

Hollywood Comes to the Alley. In 1920, the Famous Players-Lasky Corporation, a theater company, built a movie production soundstage in Astoria, about 12 miles west of Douglaston. Many early silent films were produced there, including the first two Marx Brothers comedies, *The Cocoanuts* (1929) and *Animal Crackers* (1930). In order to capture authentic scenic backdrops, filmmakers would venture beyond the studio walls and out into the neighborhoods of Queens to utilize its diverse landscape of urban, suburban, and rural—all situated within a few miles from the studio. In 1923, Paramount Pictures came to Alley Pond to make the silent film *ZaZa* with legendary actress Gloria Swanson. For the making of the movie, Buhrman's mill was transformed into a 19th-century French provincial village.

Douglaston on the Riviera. The sets for *ZaZa* were designed by Norman Norell, who also created the costumes. The studio constructed facades that would simply be placed over the existing structures in the Alley. Seen here is Buhrman's general store now transformed into a small cottage as the Alley became a massive on location set piece.

Buhrman's General Store Redux. The general store and mill are totally unrecognizable after being transformed into a cottage one would find in the French countryside. *ZaZa* was produced and directed by Allan Dwan and was a huge success for Gloria Swanson.

Douglaston on the Eve of Development. The outskirts of Douglaston are shown from the Alley, looking toward the tracks from the Port Washington Branch of the Long Island Rail Road. Numerous species of birds live within the wetlands of the Alley, including robins, blue jays, English sparrows, warblers, meadow larks, black-crowned night herons, and even quails.

THE STAGECOACH. The first recorded appearance of the stagecoach was in 1842 and was originally operated by Benjamin C. Boyd, seen in this rare photograph. At the same time, Thomas Cornwell and a Mr. Sammis ran a stage from Roslyn to Little Neck, then onto Flushing, and then lastly, Long Island City, bound for Pearl Street in Manhattan by crossing the East River using the Grand Street Ferry. The stage would leave at 8:00 a.m. daily and make its way east down Broadway (today's Northern Boulevard) toward Little Neck. The whole trip cost 25¢ to travel from Roslyn to Little Neck and 40¢ to Flushing. The full trip to the East River and then across to Manhattan cost 62.5¢. The departing location was the southeast corner of today's Little Neck Parkway and Northern Boulevard. It would also deliver mail to the Alley. The stagecoach ceased operations by 1859–1860.

THE OLD TOLLGATE. Until the 1850s, anyone traveling by stagecoach to and from Little Neck had to stop at this tollgate installed by the North Hempstead and Flushing Turnpike Road and Bridge Company. The turnpike was established after Wyant Van Zandt helped finance the construction of the causeway through the Alley, connecting Little Neck with the rest of the township of Flushing. In November 1845, flood damage to the roadway caused the years of allocated tolls to be spent on repairs and upgrades.

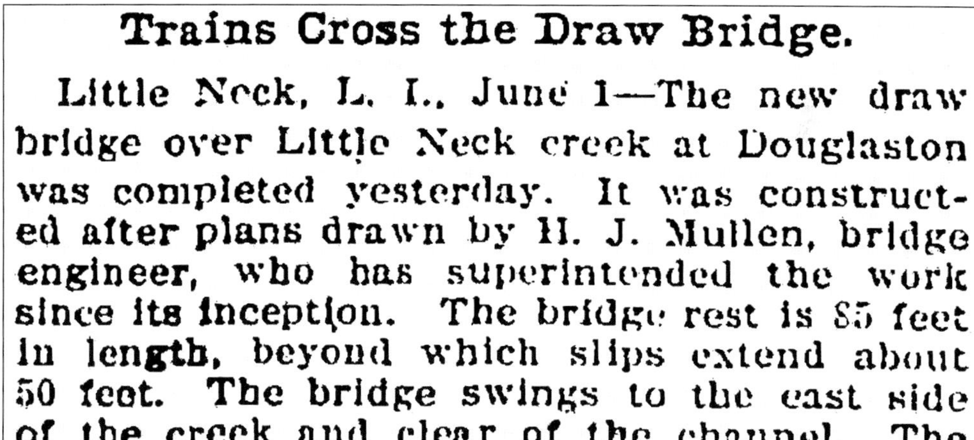

Trains Cross the Draw Bridge.

Little Neck, L. I., June 1—The new draw bridge over Little Neck creek at Douglaston was completed yesterday. It was constructed after plans drawn by H. J. Mullen, bridge engineer, who has superintended the work since its inception. The bridge rest is 85 feet in length, beyond which slips extend about 50 feet. The bridge swings to the east side of the creek and clear of the channel. The wood work which supports the iron structure and is the most important part, was constructed under the direction of J. W. Kinney, the veteran bridge carpenter of the Long Island railroad. Thursday night the new bridge was swung into position, and yesterday trains passed over it for the first time.

LONG ISLAND RAIL ROAD'S (LIRR) NEW DRAWBRIDGE. As the Flushing & North Side Railroad made its way toward Little Neck, it rendered the stagecoaches obsolete by 1860. This article published in the June 1, 1890, edition of the *Brooklyn Daily Eagle* announces the new railroad drawbridge installed by the LIRR. It was designed by H.J. Mullen and was built by J.W. Kinney. The bridge was built due to the flooding waters of the Alley, which would wash out the tracks and cause service to be delayed. Workers poured 700 loads of soil daily to help raise the height of the track bed to no avail. Thus, a bigger and more durable structure, like the drawbridge, was needed.

Van Zandt's Turnpike Upgraded. With the elimination of the stagecoach because of the Flushing & North Side Railroad, which would later be absorbed by the LIRR, another form of overland travel was needed. Travel by trolley was around the corner, and a new span, a swing bridge that could reposition itself parallel to the roadway to allow boats to pass into the bay, was erected in 1905. The bridge was built high above the waterline, providing safe and dry passage over the meadow.

Trolley Drawbridge. The swing bridge proved inadequate to support the weight of the trolley and track bed. As a result, the New York & North Shore Traction Company built a trolley drawbridge running parallel to the swing bridge, literally just a few feet away to the south. The bridge was built in two weeks and opened for service on Sunday, October 10, 1910. (New York City Records & Information Services, Eugene de Salignac Photos, Bridges/Plant & Structures.)

ONWARD INTO DOUGLASTON. The swing bridge is pictured here in 1905. Looking down Northern Boulevard (then known as Broadway), this view also focuses east toward Douglaston. On the left is D.L. Van Nostrand's (formerly Van R. Swezey) Grain, Hay, Feed, Coal & Lumber warehouse. The building would be located on what is today the Alley Pond Golf Center. The warning sign on the right informed people traveling by horse and buggy that "driving over this bridge faster than a walk is forbidden under penalty of the law!" By World War I, the number of automobiles had surpassed the number of buggies; however, their use continued well into the 1920s.

THE TROLLEY TO DOUGLASTON. The trolley of the New York & North Shore Traction Company's Flushing Division is pictured here traveling from Bayside, across the meadows of the Alley, bound for Douglaston and Little Neck with Roslyn as its final destination. The trolley came to Douglaston on September 8, 1910. The *Brooklyn Daily Eagle* reported the following day that "all Little Neck seems to have gone wild over trolleying, and there are not cars enough to carry the people who desire to ride." The trolley was powered by electricity, conducted by a guide pole on its roof that ran along wiring suspended above the roadway. Current was supplied by a power plant just a few yards away.

Little Neck Tercentenary. On Sunday, May 13, 1936, the members of the Little Neck–Douglaston Division of the Long Island Tercentenary Committee of Queens came to Buhrman's General Store in the Alley to present the "Tercentenary Commemoration Pageant of Little Neck & Douglaston." Written by Rev. Lester Leake Riley of Zion Church, the pageant featured actors in period costume (Victorian era to be exact) and was performed in front of Buhrman's General Store, which would be demolished a few months later after it stood for more than a century. Note the gristmill stone on the ground at center. "Ho! Citizens of Little Neck and Douglaston, New Yorkers all!," began the play. "I am The Chronicler! No mere mumbler of history dates am I. But the Chronicler of the romance of Little Neck, To woo you in the mimic action of our pageant—Our quaint attempt to beat the clock." Today, the colonial-era community of the Alley, home to the Buhrman homestead and Foster's Meadows, lies buried and forgotten beneath a six-lane highway. (Borough President of Queens Collection, Archives at Queens Borough Public Library.)

Three

Douglaston Is Born

William P. Douglas. It was in 1835, years before his heir would help transform the area, that a wealthy Scotsman named George Douglas came to the Little Neck peninsula and purchased the estate of Wyant Van Zandt for $30,000. A graduate of Columbia College, Douglas was a millionaire who used his fortune conservatively except when giving to philanthropic causes. Douglas was a lover of flowers and botany. He befriended famous nurseryman Samuel Parsons of Flushing, who helped transform his estate, Douglas Manor as it was called, into a botanical showcase. Douglas died in 1862 leaving his fortune to his son William Proctor Douglas, who is pictured here in 1870. The adventurous and sometimes scandal-causing heir to the Douglas fortune, William Proctor died in 1919 at age 77.

DOUGLAS MANOR. The 1819 Van Zandt–Douglas mansion went through major renovations after a fire destroyed the roof and cupola in 1921. That same year, after being used as an inn for 15 years, the home was purchased for $61,000, and a third-floor ballroom was added. It was renamed the Douglaston Club, and membership totaled 144 area residents. The private club merged with the Douglaston Yacht Squadron in 1927, which was formed with 77 members, and became the Douglaston Yacht Squadron of the Douglaston Club. The building was added to the National Register of Historic Places in 1972. It still stands today as a testament to the glory of Douglaston's origins.

SAPPHO. The racing schooner *Sappho* was purchased by William P. Douglas for $50,000 in 1868. The 28-year-old sportsman sailed the *Sappho,* constructed by Brooklyn shipbuilders Richard Poillen of C&R Poillen Bros., from New York to Queenstown, England, in 1869. The transatlantic journey took only 12 days, 9 hours, and 36 minutes, which set a record that would not be broken for 36 years. Weighing 210 tons and measuring 120 feet in length, the *Sappho* helped win the second-ever America's Cup in 1871.

DOUGLASTON'S BOTANICAL PAST. Pictured here is a seed catalog published in 1886 by Albert Benz, who operated a greenhouse in what would become Douglas Manor. An illustration of a beautiful Viola tricolor maxima graces the catalog's cover. (US Department of Agriculture.)

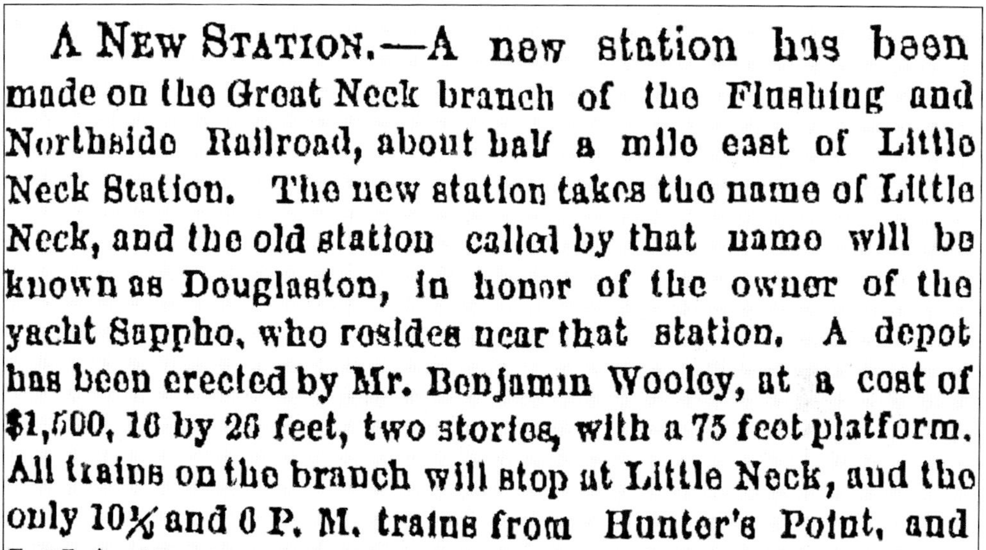

A NEW STATION.—A new station has been made on the Great Neck branch of the Flushing and Northside Railroad, about half a mile east of Little Neck Station. The new station takes the name of Little Neck, and the old station called by that name will be known as Douglaston, in honor of the owner of the yacht Sappho, who resides near that station. A depot has been erected by Mr. Benjamin Wooley, at a cost of $1,500, 16 by 26 feet, two stories, with a 75 feet platform. All trains on the branch will stop at Little Neck, and the only 10½ and 6 P. M. trains from Hunter's Point, and 7:05 A. M., 1 and 7½ P. M. from Great Neck, stop at Douglaston.

A NEW STATION ANNOUNCED. The building of a new railroad station was announced in the June 6, 1870, issue of the *Brooklyn Daily Eagle*. The article states that a new station has been built farther into the village of Little Neck and that the old station, once designated as "Little Neck," will now be called Douglaston "in honor of the owner of the yacht *Sappho*, who resides near that station." It mentions that the new station at Little Neck was built by Benjamin Wooley at a cost of $1,500. At first, all trains traveling on the Great Neck Branch (now Port Washington Branch) of the Flushing & North Side Railroad stopped at Little Neck with only two eastbound and three westbound trains stopping daily at the new Douglaston depot.

Douglaston Station. William P. Douglas commissioned the construction of this impressive Queen Anne–style station depot at a cost of $6,000 more than two decades after the first station was established. Although trains had been servicing the area since October 27, 1866, the new station was named Douglaston, officially confirming the village's name as such. Completed in June 1887, the depot housed a station master, who lived in the second-story apartment above the ticket office and waiting room. The buggy of Douglaston resident Frederick D. Stuart can be seen parked on the right. Albert Benz donated flowers from his nursery for the station's beautification.

On the Approach to Douglaston. Here is the point of view from a train on the LIRR's Port Washington Branch, as seen on February 25, 1927, approaching the Douglaston station. The castle turret of the Clinton Van Vliet mansion can be seen on the left. The tracks have been electrified, resulting in quicker service east to Long Island and west to Manhattan.

Grade Crossing, 1917. In the decades before electrification was installed between 1913 and 1917, trains on the LIRR crossed at street, or "grade," level. In many cases, there were no crossing gates to be lowered or raised. People traveling by automobile had to be very cautious of passing trains when approaching the tracks. The diamond-shaped sign reads, "Stop! Rail Road Crossing. Look Out For Cars." In the early days of cars, the railroad crossing guard would warn vehicles of an approaching train with a flag in the daytime or a lantern at night. (Vincent F. Seyfried collection.)

Station Plaza. The station plaza was constructed in the 1920s as a Tudor-style structure, which housed apartments. On the first level were several businesses, including a pharmacy and the Douglaston Delicatessen.

THE CAB STAND. As cars became the dominant form of surface transportation, it was in the 1920s that a taxi stand was installed at the Douglaston station. This photograph, taken in February 1927, shows the taxis parked in the driving circle waiting for passengers to arrive via the LIRR.

SAFE CROSSING. Crossing gates were installed in the 1920s, providing safety for automobiles as the train would come into the station.

A Final View. Looking west down the track bed, this image is of the Douglaston station crossing. Taken in the mid-1930s, one can see new passenger shelters installed on the east and westbound sides where passengers would wait for the train to arrive.

All Aboard! A rare image from 1925 shows passengers boarding the Port Washington line to head into western Queens and then finally Pennsylvania Station in Manhattan. The very stylish Queens Anne station house was deemed obsolete by the 1960s. In 1962, the green wooden-paneled station house, with its dark-brown shingled roof, was torn down and replaced by a modern one-level brick edifice. It was designed by local architect Gordon Lorimer. (Illustrations Collection–Douglaston, Archives at Queens Borough Public Library.)

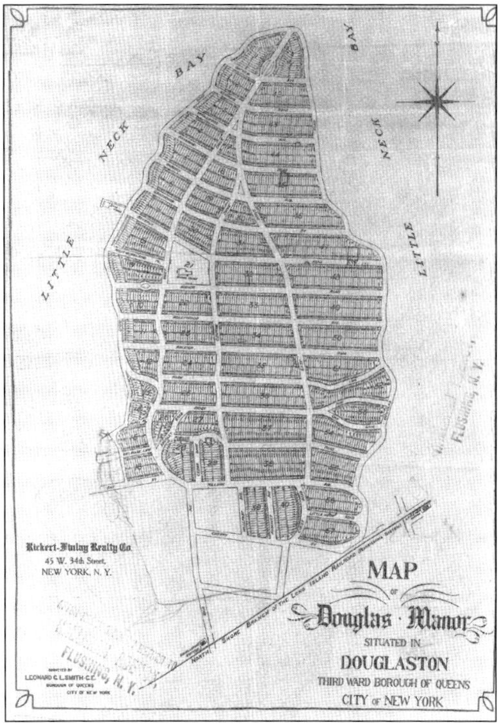

A Town, Reborn. It was in 1906 when the town of Douglaston finally came into its own, and the landscape changed forever. The Rickert-Finlay Realty Company established Douglas Manor, an exclusive enclave in a parklike setting. The development was a restricted community, meaning that there were deed restrictions to limit over development or major alterations that might threaten the original vision of the town. Where other new neighborhoods in Queens had further restrictions prohibiting persons deemed undesirable from moving in, Douglas Manor had no such restrictions.

The Rickert-Finlay Realty Company. Established by two brothers, Edward J. and Charles H. Rickert, and by Charles E. Finlay, the Rickert-Finlay Realty Company helped to establish many suburban communities in New York City, including Broadway-Flushing in Flushing and Westmoreland in Little Neck. This postcard, printed the year Douglas Manor was established in 1906, promotes the developing neighborhood boasting "2,500 restricted lots with over a mile of shore front." Upon request, the company provided free vouchers for tickets aboard the LIRR for prospective buyers to travel from crowded Manhattan or Brooklyn to come see for themselves.

ADVERTISING FOR DOUGLAS MANOR. Upon purchase of the area that was named after the estate of the Douglas family, the Rickert-Finlay Realty Company spent more than $250,000 in 1908 for the building of macadamized roads and sidewalks and the installation of water mains. Rickert-Finlay revolutionized suburban development not by selling off vacant lots but instead by building actual infrastructure first and then selling the lot with a beautifully designed home for a set price. Within the first month of the opening of Douglas Manor in the spring of 1906, the Rickert-Finlay Realty Company sold more than $1 million in homes and property.

THE DOUGLAS MANOR INN.

The Douglas Manor Inn has been sold by the Rickert-Finlay Realty Company to a syndicate organized by Charles M. Burtiss, for a consideration of $60,000. The purchasers have bought the property as an investment, and it will be continued for the present as an inn, under the same managemet. The plot occupies a entire block, and contains three acres, with a frontage of 1,275 feet on West Drive, Beverley road, Manor road and Center drive, Douglas Manor, L. I. As it is the only plot in the manor which is not restricted against the sale of liquor, and consequently the only land available for hotel uses, it is intended to improve it for that purpose.

Situated in the heart of Douglas Manor, only one block from Little Neck Bay, of which it commands one of the most beautiful views on Long Island Sound, the Douglas Manor Inn is one of the best known resorts around New York, and since its opening, four years ago, it has been a favorite resort for automobilists.

Probably no house on Long Island is of greater historic interest than the old Manor House, which was built one hundred and one years ago, and the main part of the building to-day is exactly the same as it was originally construoted. A peculiarity of its construction is that, while it is a frame building, the walls are filled with concrete, which largely accounts for its perfect condition at present.

For about sixty years previous to its purchase by the Rickert-Finlay Company, it was the home of the Douglas family, and as such was the center for the social life on the north shore. It was also the headquarters for yachting on Long Island Sound at a time when steam yachts had not been superseded by steam yachts as the favorite pleasure craft. One of the relics of these days is the foremast of the schooner Sappho, owned by the Douglas family, and which was a successful defender of the American Cup. After the yacht was dismantled, this mast was set up as a flagstaff in front of the inn, and has attracted a great deal of attention on account of its historic association.

The sale of the Douglas Manor Inn practically winds up one of the most important real estate operations on Long Island. The sales for the first thirty days following the opening by the Rickert-Finlay Company amounted to more than $1,000,000. Since this time the entire property has been thoroughly developed as a high grade residential district, miles of beautiful streets have been laid out and more than sixty artistic modern cottages have been constructed.

THE DOUGLAS MANOR INN, SOLD. When Rickert-Finlay purchased the Douglas Manor property, the company, naturally, acquired the Douglas mansion. In March 1910, the Douglas Manor mansion and its three acres were sold for $60,000 to Charles M. Burtiss. The sale of the Douglas Manor was the last major sale for the company in Douglaston, sending the profit margins of Rickert-Finlay even higher. The article shown here was printed in the March 5, 1910, edition of the *Brooklyn Daily Eagle*.

A PROMISE OF THE GOOD LIFE. This beautiful postcard advertisement reads, "We can build you a home like this in Douglas Manor, Broadway-Flushing or Westmoreland for $6,500 including land, and give you 10 years' time to pay for it!" The Rickert-Finlay Realty Company built its neighborhoods with a special contractual agreement known as a restricted covenant. This stipulation mandated that all homeowners and future developers must follow strict rules in order to preserve the architectural integrity of the homes, landscape, and overall layout of the town for all time. Such provisions included limits on how many stories a new home could have, the style of a particular home depending on which lot it was constructed, and any new building erected in the business district had to have a first story made of stone, brick, terra-cotta, or concrete.

LONG ISLAND TODAY. Douglaston's bucolic waterfront was a main attraction for many property buyers who came to the manor. Shown here is the view from Shore Drive as promoted in the 1909 history/real estate book *Long Island To-Day*, published by Hicksville resident Fredrick Ruther. The book publicized the changing landscape in the five boroughs of New York City and greater Long Island and the development of neighborhoods both old and new thanks to accessibility via automobile; the opening of the Queensborough Bridge, linking Queens and Manhattan; and improved railroad service.

Real Estate Boom. Within the first two decades of its establishment, Douglaston had become a hugely successful real estate venture. With the Rickert-Finlay Realty Company having great success in Douglas Manor, other real estate concerns began buying up tracts of land outside the manor and establishing subdivisions. Douglaston Hills was established in 1926 by H.A. Lockwood & Company, and in 1910, Douglaston Park was founded by developer J.W. Doolittle. This advertisement from 1926 shows a full-page layout of multiple listings for homes throughout the area. The advertisements show homes for price ranges between $790 and $1,150. One advertisement promises, "A Home for Every Purse and Person."

BROOKLYN DAILY EAGLE

YOU SHOULD LIVE IN

Douglaston

A town of congenial people—home owners and home lovers—situated amid beautiful surroundings, towering old trees, well-kept lawns, high elevation, rolling hills, overlooking the smooth blue waters of Little Neck Bay. Yet frequent electric express service makes the trip to and from Pennsylvania Station in 23 minutes, without change. 67 trains daily. Commutation $6.02. Restrictions—One-family type, plots ½-acre or more.

In addition to its excellent schools, churches, clubs, community tennis courts, fire and police protection, Douglaston has two bathing beaches, with more than a mile of shore front, affording ample landing and anchorage for small boats. Golf enthusiasts will revel in the fact that there are nine fine courses all within easy access.

BEST BUY ON THE NORTH SHORE

Highly restricted—every lot commands a wonderful vista. Many afford views of the Bay and Long Island Sound.

DOUGLASTON HILLS

Fully Improved at Our Expense

—PRICE—

$790 to $1,150

Easy Installment Terms

20% Down and 1½% a Month

H. A. LOCKWOOD & CO.

FIELD OFFICE: Douglaston Boulevard and Redfield Street

MAIN OFFICE: 415 Lexington Avenue New York

FROEHLICH & QUACKENBUSH, INC.

BUILDERS

Houses For Sale From $16,000 to $40,000

Assignments for Every Type of Residential Construction

Plans Executed DOUGLASTON, L. I.

HOMES BUILDING PLOTS

Douglaston Realty Co.

DEVELOPERS OF

DOUGLASTON PARK

OFFICE OPEN EVERY DAY

Northern Boulevard and Douglaston Road

DOUGLASTON

Phones Bayside 1316 or Wisconsin 6481

IDEALLY SITUATED ON THE BOULEVARD

Overlooking Little Neck Bay at

DOUGLASTON, LONG ISLAND

THEODORE WILL, BUILDER

9029 178th St., Jamaica, L. I., N. Y.

PETERSON & CO. BUILDERS

BERNARD T. JONES

A Home for Every Purse and Person

Below Are a Few of Our Representative Listings:

Office Open Evenings and Sundays

Dartmouth Rd. and Northern Blvd.

DOUGLASTON, L. I.

Douglas Manor—Douglaston Properties

HUGHES—REALTORS

DOUGLASTON At R. R. Station Main Avenue

LITTLE NECK Northern Blvd. and 248th St.

EDWIN HANSEEN

Builder of Distinctive Homes

4321 Soundview Ave., Little Neck, N. Y.

Douglaston Parkway. Originally known as Alley Road, the main thoroughfare that connects Douglas Manor with Douglaston Park is known as Douglaston Parkway. It is seen here in 1920, unpaved and rocky. The parkway is seen looking south toward the yet developed Douglaston Park, and beyond that, the Long Island Expressway (LIE) and its construction are still decades away. Note the rolling hills over which the road travels.

THE HOMES OF DOUGLASTON PARK. The photograph depicts the intersection of Alameda Avenue and 243rd Street. Douglaston Park was established in 1920. It was near this area that a group of members from the Belleclaire Country Club, located in Bayside, founded the North Hills Golf Club. The group selected this site in the Douglaston neighborhood for its rolling and scenic terrain. In 1927, the father-and-son team of landscape architects, Willie Tucker Sr. and Jr., laid an 18-hole course, named Douglaston Park, which opened on Labor Day 1927. The course features an elegant Spanish Mission–style clubhouse, designed by architect Clifford C. Wendehack.

CLINTON VAN VLIET RESIDENCE. The Clinton Van Vliet residence was built around 1899 in Douglaston. Van Vliet was president of the Goodyear Rubber Goods Company. He had begun working for Goodyear as a salesman in his early 20s and, three years later, had become its vice president. (Vincent F. Seyfried collection.)

A Home Set in Stone. The unique appearance of the house is due to Van Vliet and his collection of stones from all over the world, which he shipped back to New York and incorporated into the facade. The home also features a distinct castle-like turret. The artesian well in the front yard was also made exclusively out of these stones.

PUBLIC SCHOOL NO. 98 OF DOUGLAS MANOR. Following Clinton Van Vliet's tragic death on February 6, 1914, of gangrene, the house served as the location for Public School No. 98 until 1930, when it was demolished and replaced with a modern schoolhouse. Due to the fire code, the children's classrooms exited onto a spiral fire escape stairway on the right side of the mansion. (Bob Stonehill collection.)

PUBLIC SCHOOL NO. 98, THE DOUGLAS MANOR SCHOOL. For the 1931 school year, the city board of education constructed a modern, fireproof school building. The 1930s saw the end of the small schoolhouses scattered across the city, and one by one, they were knocked down in favor of larger, more modern, and safer buildings.

QUEENS BOROUGH MAGAZINE. First published in 1913 by the Queens Borough Chamber of Commerce, the beautifully illustrated magazine *Queens Borough* featured richly detailed articles focusing on development in every neighborhood of Queens. Shown here is an article spotlighting development in Douglaston and Little Neck in the September 1921 issue. The article celebrates the newly developed Douglaston and Little Neck areas and states, "Viewed from all angles there are few sections as attractive, and at the same time as accessible, for the tired businessman who wants to get away from the bustle of the city, and yet be in close touch with his business."

QUEENS BOROUGH
NEW YORK CITY
PUBLISHED BY THE CHAMBER OF COMMERCE OF THE BOROUGH OF QUEENS

BAYSIDE--DOUGLASTON--LITTLE NECK

Charming Residential Community Along the North Shore of Queens

The October Number will Feature the Ridgewood Section

HOMES OF THE RICKERT-FINLAY REALTY COMPANY. The Rickert-Finlay Realty Company placed this advertisement in the July 11, 1908, issue of the *Brooklyn Daily Eagle* to show the prospective home buyer the impressive types of homes that could be purchased in one of its three Queens-based communities. The communities on display here include Douglas Manor, Westmoreland, and Broadway-Flushing.

SUPERSTARS. With the Famous Players-Lasky Corporation (later Paramount) studios located just 25 minutes away in Astoria, the beautiful shorefront setting and gorgeous architecture of the homes of Douglas Manor became a huge attraction and secluded haven for some of the motion picture screen's earliest superstars. One of the first major celebrities to call Douglaston home was Ginger Rogers. A native of Missouri, Rodgers began her career on Broadway, just a half hour train ride from Douglas Manor. She rented two homes, one at 27 Richmond Road and one at 369 Beverly Road, during the summers of 1935 and 1936. Rodgers would go onto dance with Fred Astaire in many successful films, including *Flying Down to Rio* (1933), *Top Hat* (1935), and *Swing Time* (1936).

GRACE WARWICK'S SPORTS SHOP. This beautiful little boutique was situated on an island between the fork in the middle of Alameda Avenue and Northern Boulevard. The original address was No. 1 Snell Boulevard. Photographed here in 1927, the shop sold hats, dresses, and furs. (Photograph by Percy Loomis Sperr.)

A Serene Intersection. This photograph, taken on October 7, 1926, by the Queens Topographical Bureau, shows a very quiet intersection looking east on Northern Boulevard at Douglaston Parkway. The shadow of the photographers can be seen at the bottom of the picture.

Zion Church. Founded in 1830, the Zion Episcopal Church was built on a high hill on land donated by Wyant Van Zandt. Three years earlier, Van Zandt and a group of farmers gathered funds to help pay for building materials for the church. The cornerstone was laid in 1829, and the community of Little Neck helped in the physical construction. Bishop John Henry Hobart formally consecrated the small brown church on July 30, 1830. It featured a square bell tower and the churchyard. Van Zandt would pass away a year later on November 1, 1831, at the age of 66 and is buried in the family vault beneath the church. The Reverend Eli Wheeler was the church's first rector. Zion Church began holding an annual fair and strawberry festival more than 150 years ago. It still continues today.

Zion Church Portrait. The graveyard at Zion Church is the final resting place for many notable residents from Douglaston's and Little Neck's past, including the families Haviland, Allen, Cornell, Hicks, Lawrence, and Bloodgood. Even Benjamin P. Lowerre, the original owner of the general store and gristmill in the Alley, is buried here. An odd tale of Mount Zion's past occurred in the late 1860s. A group of bandits, led by Jefferson Knight, was robbing homes in Little Neck. After his arrest, he led authorities to the church where he had buried all of the stolen goods.

The "New" Zion Church. Almost a century after it opened its doors to the community, the Zion Church was destroyed in a fire in 1924. Area residents and the volunteer fire departments scrambled to put out the fire while trying to rescue priceless items of historical and religious value. The fire raced to the top of the bell tower, and soon, it broke loose from the belfry and broke into numerous fiery fragments. The rebuilding efforts began immediately with Aubrey B. Grantham, a parishioner, selected as the architect who designed a building of Colonial design. The parish house, rebuilt at the same time by another parishioner Samuel Lindbloom, was also kept to the Colonial design. Zion was rebuilt and reopened just in time for the Christmas services in 1925. The church is listed in the National Register of Historic Places.

Armenian Church. St. Sarkis Armenian Apostolic Church began service on May 20, 1962, in neighboring Bayside. On the night of May 21, 1985, the bell tower of St. Sarkis Church was hit by lightning, and the resulting fire destroyed the church. Architect Hovnan Givelekian was hired to design a new church. The ground-breaking ceremony for the new church was performed in October 1986 in Douglaston at 38–65 234th Street. On May 20, 1990, five years after the old church was destroyed, the consecration of the new St. Sarkis Church took place.

THE COMMUNITY CHURCH OF DOUGLASTON. Erected in 1924 and designed in the Colonial Revival style, the Community Church of Douglaston has served the community as a congregation of the Reformed Church in America, the country's oldest Protestant denomination. The first services were held at the Douglaston Club in 1915 before moving into a storefront church on 235th Street. A small temporary church was erected in 1919. The cornerstone of the new church was laid January 27, 1924, and the new building was dedicated on November 23 of that year. The organ was gifted in 1925 from the Women's Guild for Christian Service.

ST. ANASTASIA CHURCH. St. Anastasia Church was founded in 1915. The congregation's first church, a white wooden structure, was built in 1918 and seated 200. The first Mass celebrated there took place on May 18, 1919. The construction cost $6,000. It was torn down in 1966 and replaced with the current facility. The first pastor was Rev. John J. Clark, who served from 1916 to 1922. (Eugene L. Armbruster Photographs, Archives at Queens Borough Public Library.)

Douglaston Park. This postcard is looking south on Douglaston Avenue (now Douglaston Parkway) into the developing Douglaston Park around 1912. (Postcard Collection, Archives at Queens Borough Public Library.)

Douglaston Heights. The area of Douglaston Heights first appeared in newspapers in 1900. Seen here in a photograph from 1927 is a real estate sign for the further development of Douglaston Heights, overseen by the Lewis Development Corporation. (Eugene L. Armbruster Photographs, Archives at Queens Borough Public Library.)

Manor Apartments. Built in 1929, the Manor Apartments in historic Douglas Manor were constructed and opened for occupancy. Rentals ranged from $70 to $170. Each apartment came complete with an electric refrigerator, kitchen equipment, and a log-burning fireplace. (Illustrations Collection–Douglaston, Archives at Queens Borough Public Library.)

Building up Douglaston Park. In this rare early-1920s postcard image is the sales office for the Douglaston Park development. The office, a catty-cornered structure, was located just south of Northern Boulevard, facing Douglaston Parkway. (Bob Stonehill collection.)

THE DOUGLASTON INN. Formerly known as the Evans Hotel, the bar and restaurant became known as the Douglaston Inn. The tavern-style establishment, serving persons traveling both east and west along Northern Boulevard by automobile or by horse, was located at 244th Street and Northern Boulevard. Built in 1850, it also operated as a hotel until the 1920s, when Prohibition put an end to business. It was torn down in the mid-1930s. (Bob Stonehill collection.)

DOUGLASTON FIREHOUSE. The Douglaston Hose Company No. 1 was organized on Friday, July 10, 1903. Its firehouse was built with funds from private citizens of the town. An opening celebration was held at the Evans Hotel on July 11. A parade for the volunteers was held down Northern Boulevard where a new fire apparatus was gifted to the Douglaston volunteers. The president of the fire company was Denis O'Leary, a future US congressman. Horses originally drew the company's fire apparatus. Two decades later, the hose cart was traded for a Brockway American La France automobile hose wagon. The volunteers were disbanded in 1929 and replaced by New York City Fire Department's Hook and Ladder No. 164. The Douglaston Civic Association paid tribute to the men as they were decommissioned with the following statement: "To our own faithful volunteers we are especially appreciative of their sacrifice and devotion to the protection of our homes." (Bob Stonehill collection.)

Honoring the Fallen. The World War I monument on 235th Street was erected in 1919 and honors the 62 residents who sacrificed their lives. It was restored in 2010.

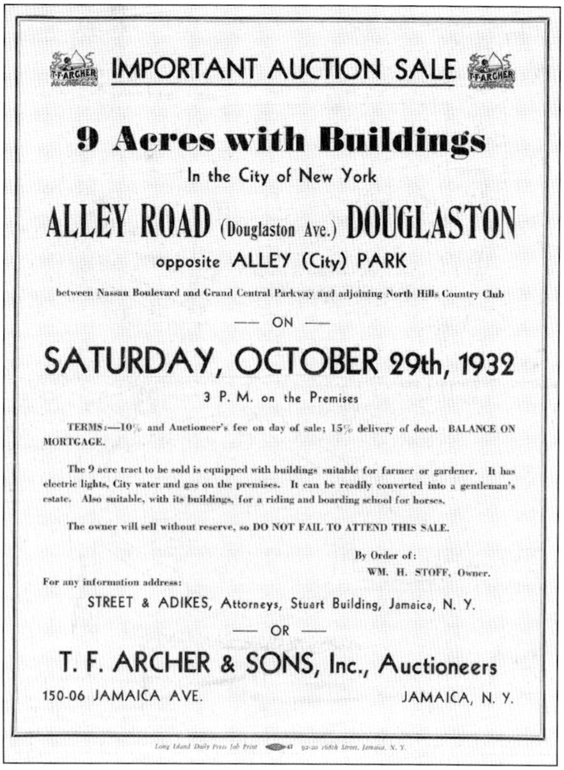

Lots for Sale. As the 20th century moved into its fourth decade, even more land became available for sale. With the Great Depression, property owners, desperately needing money, sold off their properties at auction. This rare handbill advertises a land auction on October 29, 1932, for nine acres along Douglaston Parkway (then known as Alley Road) between the Grand Central Parkway and Nassau Boulevard, today's Long Island Expressway. (Illustrations Collection–Douglaston, Archives at Queens Borough Public Library.)

Same Traffic, Different Century. Pictured on March 24, 1929, is a traffic jam at Nassau Boulevard (the Long Island Expressway) and Douglaston Parkway. Traffic became a common occurrence in the days before highways, which helped alleviate the abundance of cars on smaller roads.

The US Post Office, Douglaston Branch. Here are the letter carriers and employees of the Douglaston branch of the US Postal Service. The Douglaston branch was established in 1929. The first post office was located in the Alley. Later on, by the early 1900s, it was located in Mortiner's Café. The branch shown above was located in an alleyway, which, decades later, would be converted into an Italian restaurant, Giodino's. The restaurant is also now a part of the past. (Robert Trombley collection.)

Queens Library Douglaston Branch. The Douglaston branch of the Queens Borough Public Library opened near 243rd Street and Forty-second Avenue in 1926 with financial support from the Douglaston community. (Queens Borough Public Library Photographs, Archives at Queens Borough Public Library.)

Ladies Benefit. The women of the North Hills Golf Club staged an annual funny dress golf tournament for charity. The clubhouse can be seen in the background. The North Hills Golf Club moved out of the area in 1962.

DOUGLASTON GOLF COURSE. In 1962, the course was renamed the Douglaston Park Golf Course. Shortly before its opening, a member of the Matinecock of Little Neck performed a solemn prayer service, for, according to legend, beneath the course lies a Native American burial ground.

THE END OF THE OLD. The old powerhouse that once supplied the electrical current to the Alley's trolley system is seen here in its final days as a decaying relic of the surface traction past of Queens.

A NEW SPAN CROSSES THE MEADOWS. The old wooden bridge, which spanned the meadows for more than 50 years, was torn down, and a modern concrete span was built in 1936.

THE LIE. Members of the Queens Topographical Bureau go about their business on the day that the Long Island Expressway opened its eastern segment between Bayside and Little Neck on September 25, 1957. The new highway segment reduced the need for cars to use West Alley Road, which was known to have massive rush hour traffic.

The Douglaston Plaza. The Douglaston Plaza opened in 1962, featuring an E.J. Korvette department store. The Douglaston Korvette store was the home of a fine art gallery, which was a pet project of founder Eugene Ferkauf. It also featured a supermarket on its lower level. For more than three decades, the shopping center was home to United Artist Movieworld Theater.

THE MANOR HOUSE. In the 1960s, the United States was still enjoying the privileges of the post–World War II era. With the establishment of the new Long Island Expressway and the improvement of other arterial highway systems like the Grand Central Parkway, more and more people came to Queens from the city and from Long Island. Here is a real estate booklet for the Manor House apartment buildings, designed by Sidney and Goldhammer and developed by Borne-Chizner.

JOSEPHINE WRIGHT CHAPMAN. One of the most influential women architects of the late 19th century was Josephine Wright Chapman. Born in Fitchburg, Massachusetts, in 1867, Chapman arrived on the architecture scene around 1897 in Boston. It was there, after working for five years as an apprentice for Clarence H. Blackall, a noted designer of theaters, that Chapman started her own office at Grundman Studios as a professional architect. By 1900, she had six drafters working for her. In 1901, Chapman won a highly competitive design competition at the Pan-American Exposition in Buffalo, New York. In 1907, Chapman was accepted by the New York Society of Architects and opened her Manhattan office in Washington Square. In 1908, she brought her talents to Douglas Manor, where she designed eight homes over a nine-year period. Chapman collaborated with another woman builder named Alice Foster on five of those residences. In an interview for the *Ladies Home Journal* in 1914, Chapman commented on the relationship between builder and client. "The psychological relationship between architect and client is something that cannot readily be expressed in words," Chapman said. "In that relation I am generally able to divine just the sort of house that we will accomplish in the end." Chapman died in Bath, England in 1943.

Kiddy City. On May 1, 1954, an exciting attraction opened in an open field abutting Alley Creek on Northern Boulevard and 230th Street on the Bayside-Douglaston border. Kiddy City amusement park was an instant success, featuring rides and bumper cars. It also had an impressive 19-hole mini golf course, called Golfland. In 1956, famous roller-coaster designer Edward Leis built one out of wood called the Comet Jr. It was so popular that Kiddy City's operator, Alley Pond Amusements, added a second roller coaster made of steel years later. A fire in 1964 contributed to the shutdown of the park when Alley Pond Amusements lost its insurance and closed its doors.

Alley Pond Environmental Center. The acres of salt marsh wetlands became dumping grounds for debris from the construction of the Cross Island Parkway in the 1930s, the Long Island Expressway in the 1950s, and well into the early 1970s. The sylvan landscape of the Alley had fallen into total neglect. A group of determined educators and activists, led by Douglaston residents Hy and Joan Rosner, envisioned the damaged landscape bordering the Cross Island Parkway as a wildlife refuge and living lab for environmental education. As a result of grassroots organizing and a partnership with the Department of Parks and Recreation of New York City, the Alley Pond Environmental Center, or APEC, was established within Alley Pond Park in 1972. In 1976, APEC moved to its present location on Northern Boulevard and occupies a building that was formerly used as a furniture store.

Windmill. Standing majestically behind APEC along one of its many nature trails is this replica of the original windmill in the Alley Park–Douglaston area, which supplied water to the Douglas Manor around 1870 and stood on what is today Arleigh Road. In 1986, it was physically moved from Northern Boulevard to APEC and was burned down shortly after. With the use of private donations, the replica was built a couple years later.

The Douglaston Shopping District. This block-long, Tudor-style strip mall was built in the 1920s to serve Douglas Manor with shopping and civic and local services. The centerpiece of the structure is the former National Bank of Douglaston. The buildings were erected on the former property of Albert Benz.

The Allen-Beville House. The historic Allen-Beville House, located at 236–12 Center Drive, is one of the few surviving homes from the 19th century still standing in Douglaston. Constructed in 1847 by Benjamin Allen, the home is a classic Greek Revival farmhouse, which was popular throughout the Northeast in the 1830s and 1840s. The house is faced in clapboard and has ornate fluted Doric columns (one of the hallmarks of the Greek Revival style) and a wonderful octagonal cupola on the roof. (Photograph by author.)

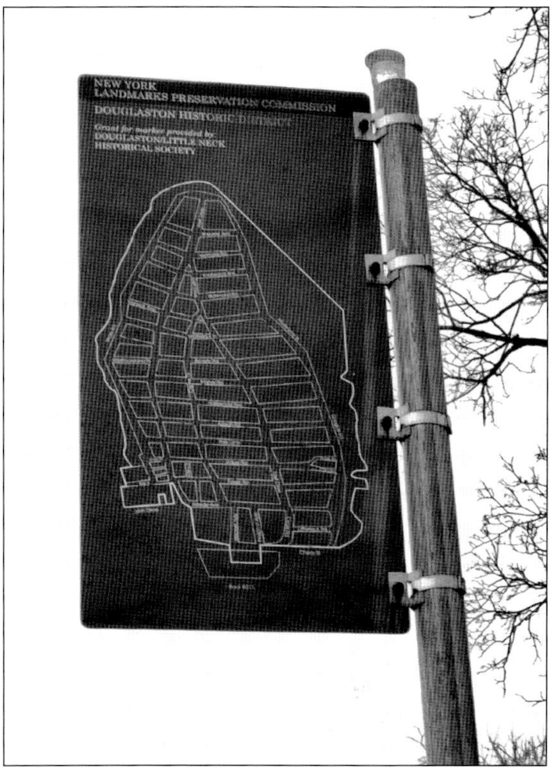

The Douglaston Historic District. Douglaston was listed in the National Register of Historic Places in 2005. In 1997, the City of New York designated Douglas Manor as the Douglaston Historic District.

AMERICAN LEGION POST NO. 103. The Little Neck–Douglaston Post No. 103 of the American Legion was originally formed on May 16, 1927. The first few monthly meetings were held in the Little Neck Firehouse at 250 Northern Boulevard and, later, at Public School No. 94 on Little Neck Parkway. The first members consisted of veterans of World War I. An application for the post's charter was drafted by residents Neal Barry, Carl Almquist, James E. Connaughton, J. Danberg, F.D. Hutton, William P. Carter, Fred Coppers, W.J. Dowd, John Simendinger, George Spindler, Harry D. Cook, Elmer C. Cornell, Daniel J. Finnegan, Charles Schmehl, and Anthony Tyson. Since 1932, Post No. 103 has met in the former firehouse of the Douglaston Hose Company. Connaughton was installed as the first commander of the post.

ST. PETER'S AME CHURCH. The former site of St. Peter's African Methodist Episcopal Church was located in a small, one-story building at the end of 243rd Street, just north of Forty-second Avenue. Founded in 1872, the congregation consisted mainly of Africa Americans, some of whom were former slaves who were then employed as oystermen in Little Neck Bay. It was a house of worship for much of the 20th century but is now a private dwelling.

George Washington Was Here. Motorists speeding down Horace Hoarding Expressway at East Hampton Boulevard on the approach to the Long Island Expressway rarely have an opportunity to notice this remarkable monument. Dedicated by the Matinecock Chapter of the Daughters of the American Revolution of Flushing on May 25, 1934, the bronze plaque, which sits upon a cloud-shaped limestone erratic, marks the spot where Pres. George Washington passed during his tour of Long Island on April 24, 1790. (Photograph by author.)

THE FAMILY MCENROE. Professional tennis legend John McEnroe grew up in Douglaston, living there for 20 years with his parents and siblings. McEnroe learned tennis at the Douglaston Club. He lived on Rushmore Avenue with his brother Mark; his mother, Kay; his father, John McEnroe Sr., a business attorney; and his other brother Patrick, who himself was also a professional tennis talent. In 1977, McEnroe and fellow Douglaston resident Mary Carillo won the mixed doubles championships at the French Open. McEnroe would play against tennis legends Jimmy Connors and Bjorn Borg. He won Wimbledon three times and won the US Open four times. (Associated Press.)

Four

Udalls Cove

A Community Activist. One of New York City's best-kept secrets and last remaining pristine wetlands was almost lost for all time when fast-spreading development threatened to destroy hundreds of acres of wetland and wooded areas. Douglaston resident Aurora Gareiss, who lived along the cove, took up the cause to save one of the finest ecological specimens located in the city limits. Located between Douglaston and Little Neck is the area known as Udalls Cove, named for resident Richard Udall in the late 1800s. In the late 1960s, there was threat of development, and the wetlands were to be filled in for a golf course. In addition, the eastern end of the Alley was slated to be developed with new houses and shopping centers. In 1969, Gareiss cofounded the Udalls Cove Preservation Committee (UCPC) along with Virginia Dent. As a direct result of their leadership work, the City and State of New York created the Udalls Cove Park and Wildlife Preserve, which extends from Northern Boulevard to Little Neck Bay. (Aurora Gareiss Papers, Archives at Queens Borough Public Library.)

Leading the Charge. In 1970, the Douglaston community began rallying to save the wetlands created by glacial runoff 15,000 years ago, which formed streams that cut into the landscape and created ravines. Years of neglect with the random dumping of garbage and even abandoned cars had hurt the ecological balance. Here are students from Public School No. 98 and area residents exploring Gabler's Creek during the "Walk in the Marsh" campaign, which invited area residents to the marshland to protest the filling of Udalls Cove by developers. The campaign was widely publicized on local television news and newspapers. (Aurora Gareiss Papers, Archives at Queens Borough Public Library.)

Reaching out to Politicians. In April 1977, New York City mayor Abraham Beame came to Udalls Cove to announce the commitment of $95,000 in city funding to help preserve the cove. Seen here are Mayor Beame (second from left), John Ried (center), and Aurora Gareiss (second from the right). (Frank Nocerito Photograph, Aurora Gareiss Papers, Archives at Queens Borough Public Library.)

Honored by the Mayor. The $95,000 in funding was approved by the city board of estimates on February 2, 1978. By that time, Edward Koch had become mayor of New York City, and it was his administration who helped push through the funding secured by his predecessor, Mayor Beame. Koch held a press conference to celebrate the approving of the funds and Udalls Cove Preservation Committee cofounders Aurora Gareiss and Virginia Dent. (Aurora Gareiss Papers, Archives at Queens Borough Public Library.)

MISSION ACCOMPLISHED. In the mid-1980s, Udalls Cove was saved and cleaned of debris and contaminants. In 1986, state senator Frank Padavan gave a proclamation to Gareiss for her 20-year commitment to help preserve the cove. Padavan was one of the many elected officials who helped preserve Udalls Cove as well as Alley Pond. Today, at the northern edge of the ravine, just south of Sand Hill Road, is Aurora Pond. This pond is named in honor for Gareiss. This body of water was created when the construction of Sand Hill Road made a dam on the northern edge of the site. Aurora Gareiss passed away in 2000 at age 91. (Aurora Gareiss Papers, Archives at Queens Borough Public Library.)

Five

Little Neck

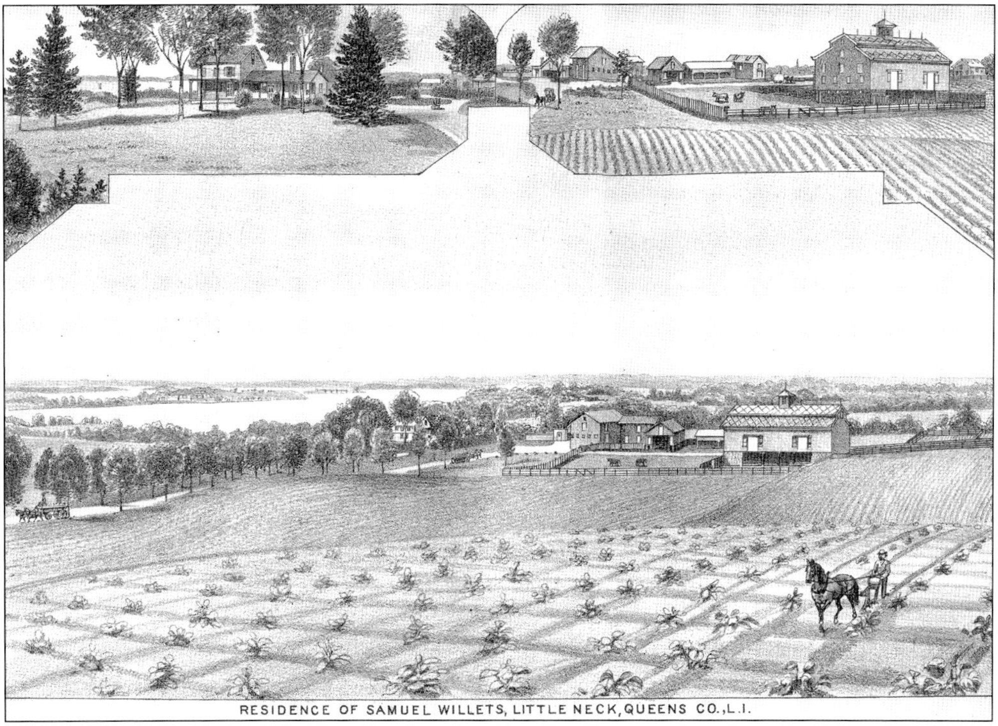

Residence of Samuel Willets. The estate of Samuel Willets, overlooking Long Island Sound, is shown here in this beautiful engraving from *History of Queens County* by W.W. Munsell, published in 1882. This panoramic scene is a beautiful example of Little Neck and the rest of Queens County's farming days. A very successful farmer, Willets was appointed president of the Queens County Agricultural Society by the State of New York in 1875, and in 1876, he was appointed overseer of highways (Northern Boulevard) by the Town of North Hempstead, for his property rested on the line between Flushing Township and the former mentioned territory. (*History of Queens County* by W.W. Munsell & Co., 1882.)

SAMUEL WILLETS. Born in Old Westbury, Long Island, on June 15, 1795, Samuel Willets made his fortune in the hardware supply business under the name A&S Willets. His other business interests included whaling, and at one time, he was part owner of 50 whaling ships. In 1869, he retired from business. He was married to Sarah Hicks from Little Neck, and she died there in 1881. Samuel Willets was also known for his philanthropic nature and gave to others so that they may start a business or farm in the area. (*History of Queens County* by W.W. Munsell & Co., 1882.)

D. L. VAN NOSTRAND.

D.L. VAN NOSTRAND. One the most notable of the earliest residents of Little Neck was David L. Van Nostrand. The owner of a building material, coal yard, and hay feed store along Northern Boulevard near the Alley and the railroad, Van Nostrand was born in Little Neck on August 30, 1851, to Albert and Harriet Van Nostrand. He began in the grocery business at the age of 17. In 1880, he was elected justice of the peace and then town supervisor of Little Neck in 1889. The Van Nostrand family first appeared in Little Neck around 1785. His estate was known as the Old Oaks, located on Northern Boulevard near Little Neck Parkway. The property extended south toward the Long Island Expressway. He died on June 3, 1913. (*History of Queens County* by W.W. Munsell & Co., 1882.)

The Walters Homestead. The homestead of G.W. Walters was located on Little Neck Parkway and Seventy-fourth Avenue on the southern border of Little Neck and Glen Oaks. The Walters property was comprised of 44 acres and was demolished in the early 1930s.

The Long Island Farmer Poet. One of the most colorful, respected residents of Little Neck is none other than Bloodgood Haviland Cutter. Born in Little Neck on August 5, 1817, Cutter was raised by his mother Mary Bloodgood. The rest of his parentage is shrouded in debate. In life, Cutter was a farmer who later married Emilline Allen, the daughter of a wealthy local farming family. Although not formerly educated, Bloodgood H. Cutter was passionate about poetry and wrote whenever he could. Most of his poems have to do with the people, places, and events of Little Neck and Douglaston and provide a unique insight into the area's history through the eyes of an artist.

The Bloodgood Homestead. When his relative Roe Haviland passed away in 1884, Bloodgood Haviland Cutter received all of his property. He built this home on the crest of a hill overlooking the Long Island Sound. He acquired more land in the coming years, including that of his wife's family. The homestead he purchased was named Allen Mill, which he renamed Cutter's Mill, the namesake of Cutter Mill Road in neighboring Great Neck. He was a respected landowner, and history has remembered him as honest with a strong acumen for business. In 1886, after an encounter with Mark Twain, he was inspired to publish a 500-page volume of his poetry, titled *The Long Island Farmer's Poems.*

THE BROOKLYN DAILY EAGLE. NEW YORK. SATURDAY. JULY 27. 1907.

OLD HOME OF POET BLOODGOOD CUTTER.

Interesting View From the Front.

Curio Contents of One of the Twenty-two Rooms.

Figurehead From Sloop the Poet Used to Sail.

been numbered and inventoried in the past few weeks and the numbers run up to over 3,000. More than three thousand articles that this eccentric genius gathered in his lifetime are to be be bid for, all the way from a stuffed weasel, so old that it is ready to fall to pieces, to the big French bedstead that looks as if it had been built for tired royalty to rest in.

The best way is to make a tour of the house as the Eagle reporter did, guided by Richard W. Smith of Lakeville, whom Mr. Cutter named as executor of his estate, and who is arranging the sale. But to go over the trip in printer's ink, make-believe, is to lose the richest part of the treat. Even a reporter's brains are not closely enough akin to his fingers to give an adequate idea of what it is like to go through the sacred chambers of the poet-farmer's lifelong home.

Neatness Not a Cutter Characteristic.

In the first place, it must be understood that Mr. Cutter was as mussy in the way he kept his things as he was queer in the way he collected them. He was one of those men who brought an article in the house, set it down wherever his convenience suggested, and thereupon christened the spot as its final resting place. It was as apt to be the floor as a mantel and a little more, and when it is recalled that he left 3,000 keepsakes behind him, it may be imagined that what he called his poetic haven of comfort and inspiration was little more than a hovel to the average housekeeper. But he loved it, and he was boss. His wife, when she was alive, used to want to tidy things up, but Cutter wouldn't let her. He said he never could find what he wanted if it were "put away," as model housewives describe their art.

After Mrs. Cutter died, Mrs. Maria Mundy kept house for him for twenty-five years—or at least she cooked his meals, and the rest of the housekeeping be tabooed. She simply had to let things alone. Cutter took pride in having things; he didn't care about having them

must have been used in Bible days and discarded when the sick were healed, and some other articles that were made before trade unions were invented.

Safe That Held a Fortune in Securities, and a Chest Full of Silver.

This is the parlor department we are in now, ladies and gentlemen, for we have come through the front hall in which stands the big safe, wherein Cutter's will and $250,000 in securities were found.

Candlesticks? Yes, right this way. Here are eleven of them in one family, all huddled together on the floor. They've been together these many, many years and are no doubt wondering now if they are going to be sold and separated like the slaves of old.

Here's a mahogany, gold inlaid table from Scotland. Start the bidding. It's got to go.

This strong box you see here was opened with great difficulty, for Mr. Cutter carried the secret of its combination to the grave with him. But after weeks of experimenting Mr. Smith, the executor, solved the problem and threw the door open. The chest was full of silver, bright as though it were new. The silverware will be sold at auction.

Here, there, everywhere in the parlor are novelties that tickle the fancy of the curious sightseer. It would be impossible to give anything like a complete list. Books? Yes, plenty of them—about 8,000 in all.

"Mr. Cutter must have been religious; here are three Bibles on the table," you say to your neighbor. Mr. Smith, who overhears you, says: "Three? Why, there are 150 in the house."

Mr. Cutter used to buy up all the old family Bibles he could get his hands on. Many of the Long Island family pedigrees can be ascertained by going through these old Bibles.

Upstairs there is a heap of small Bibles. He used to give one to every caller as a souvenir. When the Johnstown flood sufferers were in need and the people of

knocked down as bargains to folks from town.

A Chafing Dish From Jerusalem.

And, oh, girls, come and see what this is, over in the corner of the back veranda. A tin washtub? No, guess again. A patent bread pan? Wrong once more. Well, you'd never guess, so we'll have to tell you. It's a chafing dish from Jerusalem. Mr. Cutter bought it when he went on the Quaker City excursion to the Holy Land, a good many years ago, with Mark Twain. Doesn't it put the little welsh rabbit dish of yours to shame? Why, a whole family of rabbits could be cooked in this dish, but there wouldn't be much room for the lunching party if the odd looking dish were in the room.

"Here's an old rush bottom chair that ought to bring a good price," says Mr. Smith, moving a dozen other articles from it, so the visitors can get a squint at the chair itself. You take his word for it, but you've already found something else more interesting and have passed on.

"What's that I stumbled over?" you inquire, trying to regain your equilibrium, so you won't fall in a panful of old corks.

"That's a leopard's skin," says Mr. Smith.

"What, with feathers on it?"

"No, those feathers are out of an old pillow," and Mr. Smith proceeds to fan the feathers away so you can get a look at the hidden hide.

Following your guide you go up the main stairway, pulling yourself up with a rope if you like, just as the poet-farmer used to do—the tackle is still there—suddenly you enter the den, the room of all rooms in the heart of the eccentric millionaire.

In the Old Poet's Lair.

Can you pick your steps? It is a little difficult, for this room is more cluttered with rubish and relics than any other room you have seen. Here is the desk on which the "pomes" were "writ," and before it is the old arm chair that Mr.

The Cutter Homestead for Sale. In 1907, a year after Cutter's death, the *Brooklyn Daily Eagle* visited the homestead where items that belonged to Cutter, whom Mark Twain called the "Poet Lairat," were auctioned off in an estate sale. A safe with $250,000 in securities was discovered inside the home. Most of Cutter's money was donated to the Long Island Bible Society. Also inside the home, executors discovered 150 Bibles, all of which had belonged to various families throughout Little Neck and Great Neck.

Laying the Cornerstone. In August 1881, Cutter published this poem about the laying of the cornerstone at Spinney's Sunday school. The poem read as follows: "How they will here instruct the young / In Bible truths by heart and tongue, / So they may be governed by each rule / That is taught in this Sunday School."

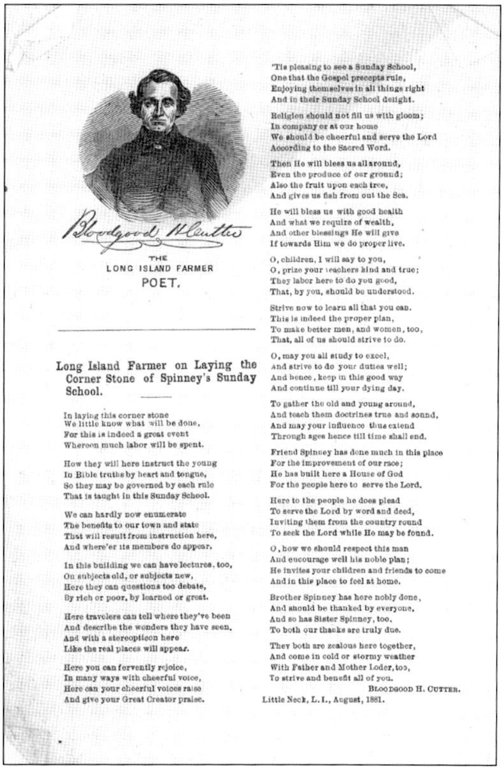

Long Island Farmer on Laying the Corner Stone of Spinney's Sunday School.

In laying this corner stone
We little know what will be done,
For this is indeed a great event
Whereon much labor will be spent.

How they will here instruct the young
In Bible truths by heart and tongue,
So they may be governed by each rule
That is taught in this Sunday School.

We can hardly now enumerate
The benefits to our town and state
That will result from instruction here,
And where'er its members do appear.

In this building we can have lectures, too,
On subjects old, or subjects new,
Here they can questions too debate,
By rich or poor, by learned or great.

Here travelers can tell where they've been
And describe the wonders they have seen,
And with a stereopticon here
Like the real places will appear.

Here you can fervently rejoice,
In many ways with cheerful voice,
Here can your cheerful voices raise
And give your Great Creator praise.

'Tis pleasing to see a Sunday School,
One that the Gospel precepts rule,
Enjoying themselves in all things right
And in their Sunday School delight.

Religion should not fill us with gloom;
In company or at our home
We should be cheerful and serve the Lord
According to the Sacred Word.

Then He will bless us all around,
Even the produce of our ground;
Also the fruit upon each tree,
And gives us fish from out the Sea.

He will bless us with good health
And what we require of wealth,
And other blessings He will give
If towards Him we do proper live.

O, children, I will say to you,
O, prize your teachers kind and true;
They labor here to do you good,
That, by you, should be understood.

Strive now to learn all that you can.
This is indeed the proper plan,
To make better men, and women, too,
That, all of us should strive to do.

O, may you all study to excel,
And strive to do your duties well;
And hence, keep in this good way
And continue till your dying day.

To gather the old and young around,
And teach them doctrines true and sound,
And may your influence thus extend
Through ages hence till time shall end.

Friend Spinney has done much in this place
For the improvement of our race;
He has built here a House of God
For the people here to serve the Lord.

Here to the people he does plead
To serve the Lord by word and deed,
Inviting them from the country round
To seek the Lord while He may be found.

O, how we should respect this man
And encourage well his noble plan;
He invites your children and friends to come
And in this place to feel at home.

Brother Spinney has here nobly done,
And should be thanked by everyone,
And so has Sister Spinney, too,
To both our thanks are truly due.

They both are zealous here together,
And come in cold or stormy weather
With Father and Mother Loder, too,
To strive and benefit all of you.

Bloodgood H. Cutter.

Little Neck, L. I., August, 1881.

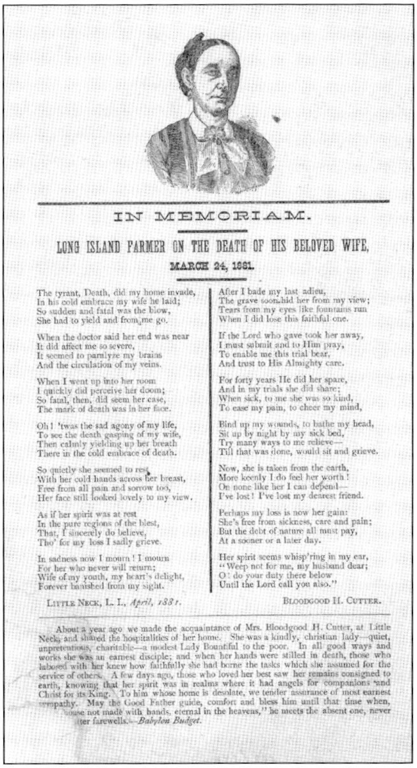

IN MEMORIAM.

LONG ISLAND FARMER ON THE DEATH OF HIS BELOVED WIFE,

MARCH 24, 1881.

The tyrant, Death, did my home invade,
In his cold embrace my wife he laid;
So sudden and fatal was the blow,
She had to yield and from me go.

When the doctor said her end was near
It did affect me so severe,
It seemed to paralyze my brains
And the circulation of my veins.

When I went up into her room
I quickly did perceive her doom;
So fatal, then, did seem her case,
The mark of death was in her face.

Oh! 'twas the sad agony of my life,
To see the death gasping of my wife,
Then calmly yielding up her breath
There in the cold embrace of death.

So quietly she seemed to rest,
With her cold hands across her breast,
Free from all pain and sorrow too,
Her face still looked lovely to my view.

As if her spirit was at rest
In the pure regions of the blest,
That, I sincerely do believe,
Tho' for my loss I sadly grieve.

In sadness now I mourn! I mourn
For her who never will return;
Wife of my youth, my heart's delight,
Forever banished from my sight.

After I bade my last adieu,
The grave soon hid her from my view;
Tears from my eyes like fountains run
When I did lose this faithful one.

If the Lord who gave took her away,
I must submit and to Him pray,
To enable me this trial bear,
And trust to His Almighty care.

For forty years He did her spare,
And in my trials she did share;
When sick, to me she was so kind,
To ease my pain, to cheer my mind,

Bind up my wounds, to bathe my head,
Sit up by night by my sick bed,
Try many ways to me relieve—
Till that was done, would sit and grieve.

Now, she is taken from the earth,
More keenly I do feel her worth!
On none like her I can depend—
I've lost! I've lost my dearest friend.

Perhaps my loss is now her gain:
She's free from sickness, care and pain;
But the debt of nature all must pay,
At a sooner or a later day.

Her spirit seems whisp'ring in my ear,
"Weep not for me, my husband dear;
O! do your duty there below
Until the Lord call you also."

Little Neck, L. I., *April, 1881*.

Bloodgood H. Cutter.

About a year ago we made the acquaintance of Mrs. Bloodgood H. Cutter, at Little Neck, and shared the hospitalities of her home. She was a kindly, christian lady—quiet, unpretentious, charitable—a modest Lady Bountiful to the poor. In all good ways and works she was an earnest disciple; and when her hands were stilled in death, those who labored with her knew how faithfully she had borne the tasks which she assumed for the service of others. A few days ago, those who loved her best saw her remains consigned to earth, knowing that her spirit was in realms where it had angels for companions and Christ for its King. To him whose home is desolate, we tender assurance of most earnest sympathy. May the Good Father guide, comfort and bless him until that time when, [illegible]ouse not made with hands, eternal in the heavens," he meets the absent one, never [illegible]ter farewells.—*Babylon Budget*.

In Memoriam. When his wife, Emilline Allen, died on March 24, 1881, Cutter wrote a memorial poem, which was published in the newspaper, the *Babylon Budget*. "In sadness now I mourn! I mourn / For her who never will return; / Wife of my youth, my heart's delight, / forever banished from my sight," lamented Cutter in the poem, which he titled *In Memoriam*.

The Late B.H. Cutter. At the age of 89, Cutter died in September 1906. He is best remembered by his book of poems and by his mentioning in Mark Twain's great American novel *Innocents Abroad* in which Cutter is portrayed as "Poet Lariat." Cutter and Twain met by accident on the same vessel while sailing to the Holy Land in 1867. The following is how Twain described Cutter: "He is 50 years old, and small for his age. He dresses in homespun, and is a simple minded old fashioned farmer with a strange proclivity for writing rhymes. He writes them on all possible subjects and gets them printed on slips of paper with his portrait at the head. These he will give to any man that comes along, whether he has anything against him or not."

The Decline of Cutter's Mill. The property of Cutter's Mill was developed by the late 1920s. The eastern part of his estate became virtually of all of the Terrace Circle Apartments in Nassau County, Long Island, not too far from the Little Neck border. A year before his death on the occasion of his 88th birthday, Cutter wrote, "Bloody Cutter is eighty-eight, Obeying God and defying Fate, He lives in Little Neck town, His age goes up, not down." Pictured here is Cutter's grave at Zion Church.

FOURTH OF JULY FETE GIVEN BY BENJAMIN WOOD, ESQ., AT HIS SUBURBAN RESIDENCE, NEAR LITTLE NECK BAY, LONG ISLAND—ILLUMINATION AND FIREWORKS.—SEE PAGE 138.

FOURTH OF JULY AT BENJAMIN WOOD'S. A beautiful depiction of life in mid-19th century Little Neck, these wood engraved views were featured in *Frank Leslie's Illustrated Newspaper* on July 21, 1860, showing the Fourth of July celebration at the residence of Benjamin Wood, Esq. The accompanying article reads as follows: "It has been the practice of Mr. Wood for many years past, to throw open his beautiful grounds on the night of our great National Birthday, for the amusement of his friends and neighbors. It is an invitation understood by all, and thousands availed themselves of it in the occasion, and passed a few hours of uninterrupted enjoyment. We, among others, turned our steps to the Long Island Mecca, and after a delightful ride of fourteen miles, passing through the pretty town of Flushing and a beautiful country, we arrived at the elegant grounds and villa of the popular and courteous host, Benjamin Wood, Esq. The grounds consist of a homestead of over sixty acres of the most fertile and productive land, finely wooded and replete with features of beauty."

EWORKS ON BENJAMIN WOOD'S GROUNDS—"LONG ISLAND."

BANQUET UNDER THE TENT IN MR. WOOD'S GROUNDS.

Fireworks on Display. The next few engravings from the same issue of *Frank Leslie's Illustrated Newspaper* show the Fourth of July banquet under the tent on the grounds of the Wood estate. The stud stable was a main attraction for guests at the party, and when the evening came, it was time for fireworks with some spelling out "Long Island" and "Welcome to All."

ROAD ACCIDENT.—On Sunday afternoon two unknown gentlemen were seen seated in a buggy, behind a spirited horse, tearing along the road in the vicinity of Andrew Lynch's hostleric at Little Neck, and, while descending the hill, just before reaching the toll-house, one of them was thrown from the vehicle, in consequence of one of the wheels coming in contact with a gate-post, and, falling on his head, broke his neck, causing his death in a few moments.

A TERRIBLE ACCIDENT. Life in Little Neck two centuries ago came with hazards no different from the ones people encounter today. Especially with regard to vehicular traffic and road conditions. This article from the *Brooklyn Daily Eagle*, published on May 14, 1867, reports an accident involving two men driving a buggy along Northern Boulevard. Upon reaching the tollhouse in the Alley, the horse sped up and could not be slowed down. The buggy struck the side of the gate and ejected one of the passengers who broke his neck and died on the scene. The accident happened near Andrew Lynch's hostelry.

FIRE AT LITTLE NECK.—Yesterday morning, a fire broke out at Little Neck Village, burning a distillery house and shoemaker's shop belonging to James Graham, and a large barn and shed, the property of E. C. Poole. As there was no fire department convenient nothing could be done to save the property. The barn was full of hay, and Mr. Poole lost from $2,000 to $2,500. Mr. Graham's loss is about $1,000. On the barn there was an insurance of $500.

MORE BAD NEWS. On July 6, 1870, a fire broke out in the shop of James Graham, the village shoemaker, and spread next door to the barn and shed of E.C. Poole. There were no injuries, but the cost of the damages to both parties came to $3,500. A more serious incident, worse than loss of property, befell Graham less than three years later.

MYSTERIOUS MURDER.

A Little Neck Shoe Dealer Killed by a Customer.

A mysterious murder has been perpetrated at Little Neck, L. I. The victim, James Graham by name, was a shoe dealer, who did quite an extensive business in Little Neck. He was known as a quiet, industrious man. For fifteen years he had been a resident of the village, and in that time had accumulated about $15,000, most of which was invested in real estate. Not long since his store and workshop were burned down, which led to the erection of the building in which he met his death.

On Saturday morning a boy called at Graham's store to have his shoe mended. As he stepped in he was almost paralyzed at the sight which met his gaze. In

A POOL OF BLOOD

Graham lay dead, his eyes wide open, his head gashed frightfully. The boy fled in terror. The body was shortly after taken in charge by Coroner Reimer.

A close inspection of the murdered man's wounds showed that he had received a deep cut about four inches in length across the forehead, the weapon having penetrated the bone, two very deep wounds, one on each temple, and a cut right between the eyebrows which looked as though a weapon had pierced the skin just above the nose and come out at the bridge of the nose. The head was also bruised, where it came in contact with the brown porcelain knob of the door, and the knob was broken in two pieces, which lay at some distance from each other. The wounds had bled copiously, and the dead man's clothes were saturated. There was a pool of blood near his head, and, as above stated, he had evidently been looking upon this blood while dying. In one hand he held a piece of brown wrapping paper, and the boot lying near him he had evidently used in vain defense of his life. Not only the clothing of the murdered man, but the boot, the wall, and the open door were spattered with blood, indicating that he had not yielded without a struggle

THE MURDER OF JAMES GRAHAM. On February 7, 1873, shoemaker James Graham was busy working in his newly rebuilt shoe shop. Sometime just before noon, a young unidentified man came to have his shoes repaired. He found Graham on the floor with his head bashed in and eyes wide open. Graham did not go down without a fight, using one the boots he was repairing as a weapon against his attacker. No suspect was ever charged with the murder.

LITTLE NECK BUSINESS DIRECTORY, 1891. Lain's 1891 Long Island Business Directory shows the types of professions in existence almost a century and a half ago. The names of Little Neck's notable residents and families, including David L. Van Nostrand and the Cornell, Cutter, Foster, Fowler, Hicks, Remsen, and Schenck families, are listed here. The town butcher was Hazard & Vrendenburgh, and the village blacksmiths were John Bennem and Michael P. Welsh.

JAY STREET, BROOKLY

Little Neck.

POST OFFICE, Benjamin W. Schenck, Postmaster.
CONSTABLE, George Roe.
HIGHWAY COMMISSIONER, William L. Cornell.
SUPERVISOR, David L. Van Nostrand.
CHURCHES, *Epis.*, Re . Edgar L. Sanford; Union.
PUBLIC SCHOOL, District No. 1, N. F. Mosher, Prin.
SCHOOL TAX COLLECTOR, George W. Hutton.
SCHOOL TRUSTEES, Benjamin W. Schenck, John Bennem and David L. Van Nostrand.
EXCELSIOR BRASS BAND.

AGENT, INSURANCE.

Morgan George C.

AGRICULTURAL IMPLEMENTS.

Van Nostrand David L.

BLACKSMITHS.

Bennem John
Welsh Michael P.

BOARDING HOUSE.

Louzin Nicholas

BOOTS AND SHOES.

Venzke Herman

BUILDING MATERIALS.

Van Nostrand David L.

BUTCHERS.

Hazard & Vredenburgh

CARPENTERS.

Black Malcom A.
Cornell George H.

CARRIAGE MAKER.

Wright Alfred P.

COAL AND WOOD.

Van Nostrand David L.

FARMERS.

Anderson John
Cobb John
Conklin Jeremiah
Cornell Charles W.
Cornell Henry B.
Cornell John
Cornell William L.
Coughlin John
Cox Henry
Cutter Bloodgood H.
Foster John
Fowler Benjamin Mrs.
Fowler James
Gill George H.
Herrick John
Hicks John
Hicks Ruscom S.
Jagnow Bros.
Kissam William A.
Louzin Nicholas
Payne George W.
Place William H.
Poole Isaac
Reed John
Remsen John R.
Schenck Daniel R.
Sutphen George R.
Thurston John
Van Nostrand Albert
Van Nostrand Wm. H.
Van Nostrand Wm. L.
Walters Charles W.
Woolley Benjamin W.

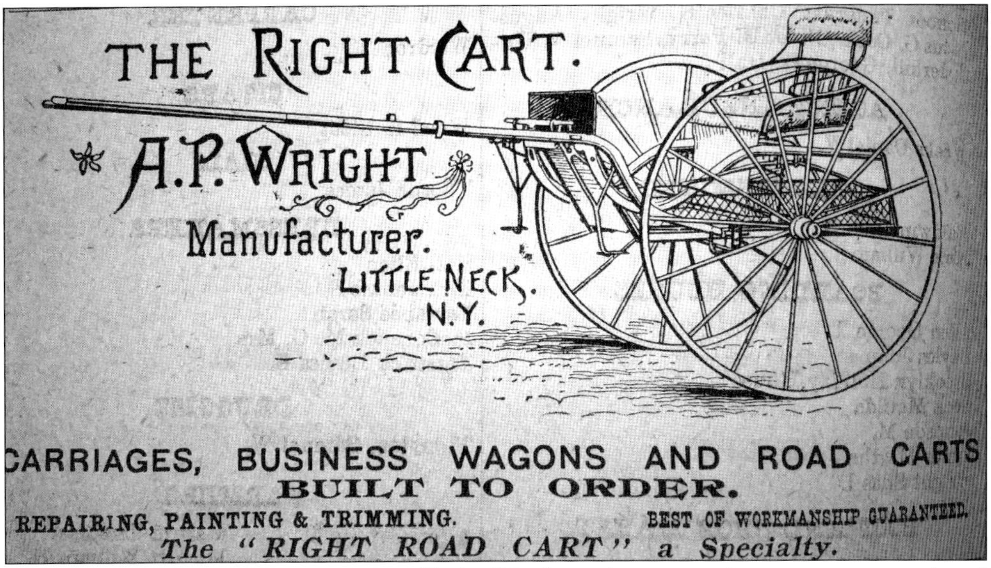

ALFRED P. WRIGHT, CARRIAGE-MAKER. Alfred P. Wright made carriages, business wagons, and road carts. This 1891 advertisement for A.P. Wright's wagon shop promises customers "the right cart."

THE WORKSHOP OF A.P. WRIGHT. A very successful businessman in the village, Alfred P. Wright operated a wheelwright shop on the north side of Northern Boulevard between Marathon Parkway and Cornell Lane. The grandson of Benjamin P. Lowerre, Wright was born in Brooklyn on August 27, 1849. Wright started his wagon business at age 19. In business for more than 40 years, Wright gave up his horse-drawn wagon shop with the advent of the automobile. Another notable product that he helped manufacture from his workshop were clam rakes. Made with heavy iron prongs fitted to long wooden handles, these rakes were sold to local clamdiggers. Wright made wagons for William P. Douglas and Judge H.S. Moore. He also made hansom cabs, which were popular in the mid-1800s, as they were designed to combine speed with safety with a low center of gravity for safer turns. (Bob Stonehill collection.)

Photographs of Edgar E. Rutter. The next four photographs were taken by Edgar E. Rutter, a professional photographer of New York streetscapes and official photographer for Brooklyn. Rutter took these images of old homesteads along Little Neck Parkway on March 19, 1931. These cottages were constructed in the 1850s. Here is the original homestead of the Marvin family.

J. Benham Homestead. In the last years of the 19th century, this home belonged to J. Benham. It was originally used as a schoolhouse. The home was located on Little Neck Parkway just before the southwest corner of Northern Boulevard.

OLD J. THORNELL FAMILY PROPERTY. Here, an old farmhouse is located on the J. Thornell family acreage. The home is depicted abandoned in what is probably the last-known image before its demise for the development of the Westmoreland neighborhood subdivision.

BARON-WATERS PROPERTIES. Looking southbound on Little Neck Parkway, one can see the Baron and Waters family property on the right. Most of these homes have belonged in their family for almost two centuries. The Baron and Waters families are direct descendants of Long Island Native American peoples. The property line was also shared by Benjamin Woolley.

Alfred P. Wright Homestead. Here is the Alfred P. Wright home. It was built in 1869 on Northern Boulevard before being moved farther back from the roadway in the early 1930s.

Looking for Clams. These men are seen here searching or raking for clams in Little Neck Bay in 1897. It is from this very area where Little Neck clams get their namesake.

Frank Jackowski, Farmer. In the foreground is Frank Jackowski with his family and laborers. Note the horse-drawn plows working hard in the background. Jackowski's farm was located on Clinton Avenue (today's Marathon Parkway) just south of Van Zandt Avenue. Percy Loomis Sperr, the official photographer for New York City, took this photograph on June 10, 1927, during a visit to Little Neck. (Percy Loomis Sperr collection.)

Little Neck Parkway and Broadway. This never-before-published photograph from 1913 shows the intersection of Little Neck Parkway and Northern Boulevard. To the left is the Little Neck Hotel, owned by P. Moser. On the right is the general store, built by Edgar C. Poole in 1861. The store sold everything from clothes and shoes to food, kerosene, and oil lanterns. Poole later sold it to Walters and Schenck. Walters later sold his share to Van Nostrand. In 1895, George Howe purchased it and operated it as a Grand Union Tea Company store.

Little Neck's First School. Located on the northeast corner of Bates Road and Little Neck Parkway, this two-room schoolhouse was erected in 1865 on property donated by John Cornell. In 1898, after the consolidation of the five boroughs, the city took over the school and added several rooms, designating it Public School No. 32. The school had no electricity, and students got water for drinking from a well. It was closed in 1914. (Percy Loomis Sperr collection.)

THE WATERS HOMESTEAD. The Waters homestead was built in the early 1800s on Little Neck Parkway just north of Northern Boulevard. The two-story home featured a well in the backyard, which provided fresh water to all those in the community who needed it. The postcard playfully reads, "No, No Trespass sign here to chase away the thirsty wayfarer." The Waters family is one of the area's most historic families. Their descendants continue to reside in Little Neck to this day. (Bob Stonehill collection.)

THE WHITE MAN'S BARGAIN STORE. Owned by M. White of Little Neck around 1900, the property on the Waters homestead was used as a general store. A sign for Horton's Ice Cream is out front. (Bob Stonehill collection.)

CORNELL'S LITTLE NECK GARAGE. Since the early 1700s, the Cornell family lived in Little Neck on a homestead of 1,000 acres, which was granted onto them from England. Their property ran from Northern Boulevard all the way south to Jericho Turnpike. One property deed, dated October 20, 1772, mentions that the property where one Joseph Cornell lived was parted by a highway that leads from the Great Plains to Little Neck. This "highway" is today's Little Neck Parkway. The property of William H. Cornell, which is the main homestead of the Cornell family, was situated on the east side of Little Neck Parkway about 100 yards north of the Long Island Expressway at 54–47 Little Neck Parkway. (Bob Stonehill collection.)

Six

THE RAILROAD AND PUBLIC SERVICES

BUILDING THE LINE TOWARD LITTLE NECK. The Flushing & North Side Railroad was established on April 3, 1868, and absorbed the Great Neck Line, which had operated briefly under the North Shore Railroad and then the New York & Flushing Railroad lines. Tracks were laid out to Douglaston in October 1866. The station had the original designation of Little Neck but was physically moved to Little Neck Village once the western part of the area became known as Douglaston. William P. Douglas helped erect a new station house in 1887. He had the original station house relocated where it still stands today as a private residence on Jessie Court. Workers are seen here laying down tracks toward the new station in Little Neck proper.

The Approach to Little Neck Station. The new station, shown here, now had the official designation of Little Neck and was built by Benjamin Wooley at a cost of $1,500. The station opened in July 1870 with a 75-foot-long platform. The fare to travel to Pennsylvania Station cost 41¢. Additions were made to the building in 1890. The Great Neck Line was redesignated as the Port Washington Branch in 1902.

Little Neck Station. Here is another view of the station in 1940. The Little Neck depot included a taxi stand and a Western Union office and featured a potbelly stove in the center of the waiting room to keep travelers warm during the harsh Long Island winters.

Electrification. As part of the Long Island Rail Road's grade crossing safety program, almost all branches received electrified rail service with the instillation of a third rail carrying 600 volts of electricity, thus eliminating the days of the steam locomotive. Tracks were depressed below ground or ran on an elevated track bed so pedestrians would not be hurt by the deadly electrified rail. During this project, more than 270,000 cubic yards of earth were moved, and 61,000 yards of concrete wall were built. Little Neck station features one of the few surface crossings in Queens. The third rail is protected by a metal plate and runs beneath the passenger platform on both west and east sides.

Across the Wire. Press Wireless Corp. was founded in 1929 to help transit news briefings and real-time information for several prominent news agencies, including the *Chicago Daily News*, *New York Times*, *Associated Press*, *New York Tribune*, *Christian Science Publishing*, and *King Features Syndicate* to name a few. Known in its abbreviated term as PreWi, the press wireless receiving stations were set up all over Long Island to help relay real-time news information "over the wire." The receiving station at Little Neck, located near the LIRR, was in constant use until the late 1940s. The transmitting site opened for full service in 1932. By 1933, the company had five call signs—WJO, WJP, WJQ, WJS, and WJU.

THE ORIGINAL LITTLE NECK STATION. Situated at the end of Jessie Court, one of the oldest streets in Queens, is the original Little Neck station house, which was placed on this site by William P. Douglas more than 150 years ago. The station was built from April to May 1867. In June 1870, it was updated with a freight platform, and a second story was added in the summer of 1871. Today, it sits hidden along this narrow street, which looks like a driveway leading north from Northern Boulevard. One of the many secrets of Little Neck's past still in existence yet tucked away out of sight. The relocation of the old station, situated in the middle of the row of houses, is still debated by historians.

VANDERBILT CUP RACE. The Vanderbilt Cup was the first auto racing competition in America. Started by William Kissam Vanderbilt, the inaugural season began on October 8, 1904. The 1906 Vanderbilt Cup race, depicted here just outside Little Neck, faced a new course layout. The construction of the trolley line stretching from Long Island City to Mineola in Nassau County forced a redesign of the western section of the course from its original 1905 course layout. In all, the course presented 11 turns per lap or a total of 110 during the 10-lap, 297-mile race.

Little Neck Fire Volunteers. One of the most historic events of Little Neck occurred with the establishment of a volunteer firefighting service. Since most of the homes and businesses in Little Neck were still wood-framed structures at the start of the 1900s, fires were a regular occurrence, resulting in costly damages and loss of life. A volunteer firefighting company was the only answer. In February 1901, the Active Hook, Ladder & Hose Company No. 1 was established. It was notable local businessman David L. Van Nostrand who donated his property so that a temporary firehouse could be built. The new permanent firehouse, seen above, was finally completed in 1905 and staffed by 60 volunteers.

The Firehouse for Active Hook, Ladder & Hose Co. No. 1. At the time of its establishment, Active Hook, Ladder & Hose Company No. 1 fought fires with the use of a fire apparatus. It included a hand pump and water buckets made of leather, which were used to carry water from streams or wells on nearby properties to help battle the blaze. The apparatus, which was originally pulled by hand, was later drawn by horses. The firehouse was built based on plans drawn by resident Isaac P. Robinson and was constructed by George W. Cornell.

Little Neck Firehouse in Later Years. The firehouse for the Active Hook, Ladder & Hose Company No. 1 is seen here in April 1927, two years before its closing. Townspeople used the bell tower to notify the volunteers that a fire was in progress and that their immediate attention was needed. This system was necessary because no modern-day fire alarm system had been created at the time of the company's creation in 1901. (Eugene L. Armbruster Photographs, Archives at Queens Borough Pubic Library.)

The Last Call. On Saturday, November 30, 1929, the brave men of the Little Neck volunteer fire company joined numerous other volunteer companies from neighboring Douglaston, Great Neck, Port Washington, Manhasset, and Lakeville in a parade welcoming the arrival of the New York City Fire Department, which, of course, is a paid fire company. The volunteers were mustered out as the companies of Douglaston and Little Neck ended a 28-year run. Engine No. 313 and Hook & Ladder No. 164 took their place. Speakers at the event included New York City mayor James J. Walker, New York City fire commissioner John J. Dorman, and Queens Borough president George U. Harvey. The firehouse, located at the northeast corner of Marathon Parkway and Northern Boulevard, was torn down in the fall of 1969.

Seven

Little Neck Comes of Age

Little Neck's Farming Days. Long before the establishment of Douglaston and its historic Douglas Manor, there was the town of Little Neck. Located at the northeastern frontier of Queens County, the village was mainly a rural farming community until the beginning of the 1920s, when development throughout the borough exploded and Queens made its long transition from farmland and open fields to both developed and planned communities bisected by major highways and thoroughfares. Shown here is a farmer tending to his crops at what is today the intersection of Marathon Parkway and Sixtieth Avenue. (Percy Loomis Sperr collection.)

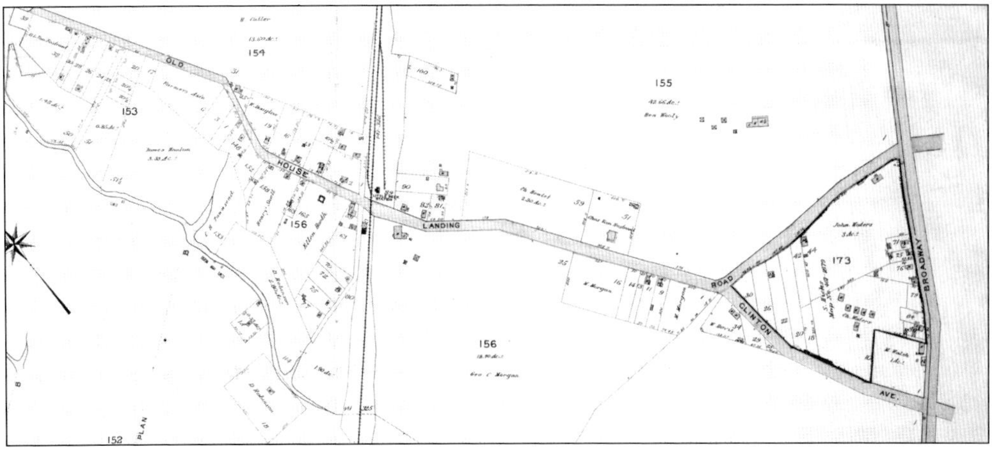

EARLY MAP OF LITTLE NECK. This 1904 map shows Little Neck (part of the Third Ward of Queens County). At this time, Marathon Parkway was known as Clinton Avenue, and Little Neck Parkway was known as Old House Landing Road. This plate from an E. Belcher Hyde atlas of Queens shows the property of John Waters and Thomas Hicks, who both owned the majority of the property that makes up the triangular wedge bounded by Clinton Avenue, Old Landing House Road, and Broadway.

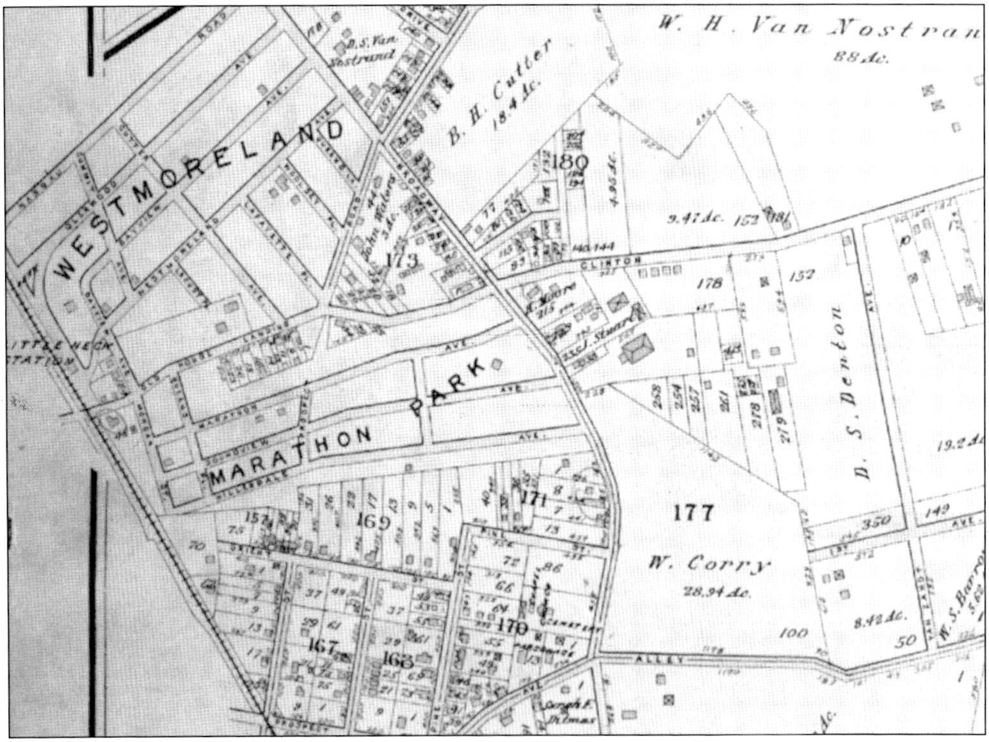

DEVELOPING LITTLE NECK. This Beers map from 1909 shows the establishment of Westmoreland and Marathon Park north of Northern Boulevard. These communities would eventually expand south of the boulevard in the coming years. Note how, although both areas are labeled with the names of the neighborhoods and streets and lots have been established, there are no homes yet built on them. The properties bearing the names of W.H. Van Nostrand and Bloodgood Haviland Cutter can be seen on the right.

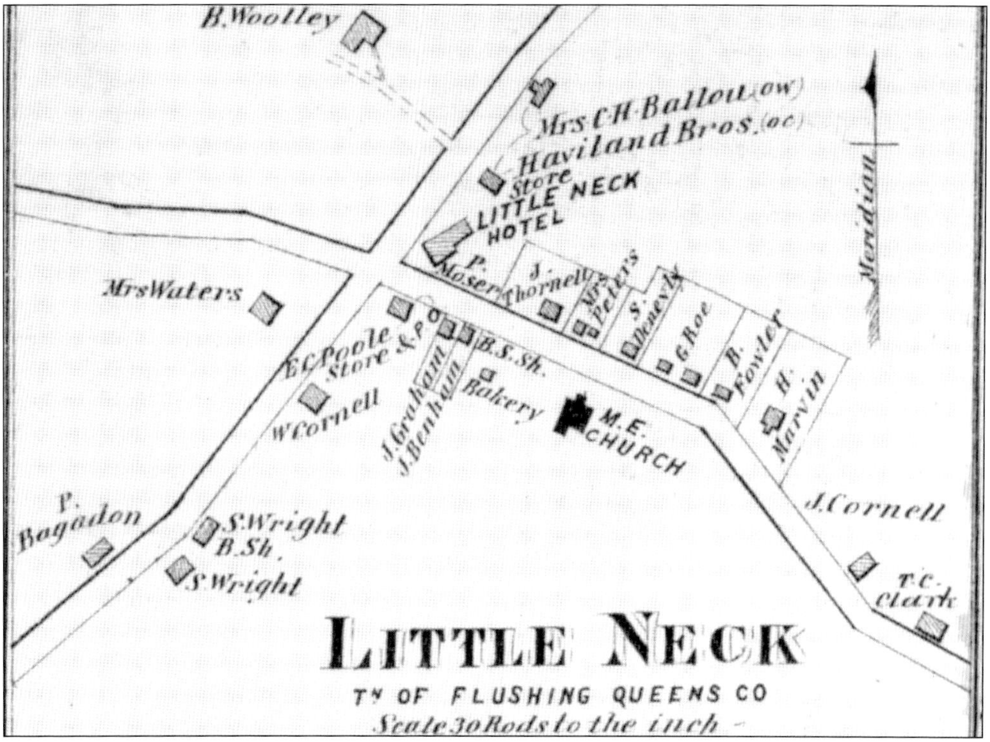

Little Neck in 1873. The heart of the business area of Little Neck is seen here in detail in this 1873 map by Frederick W. Beers. The general store of E.C. Poole, which also housed the post office, can be seen at the southwest corner of Northern Boulevard and Little Neck Parkway. Opposite the general store is the Little Neck Hotel owned by P. Moser.

A View of Little Neck. This October 19, 1922, photograph is of Little Neck as seen from Mickle Pond, looking across Little Neck Bay. Located in neighboring Bayside, the property overlooking the bay belonged to Andrew Mickle. The son of immigrants from Scotland, Mickle made his fortune as a tobacco merchant in Manhattan and served as the mayor of New York City for half of one term. After his two-year stint from 1846 to 1847, he came to Bayside and established a mansion in Bayside Lawn, which is today's Cunningham Park.

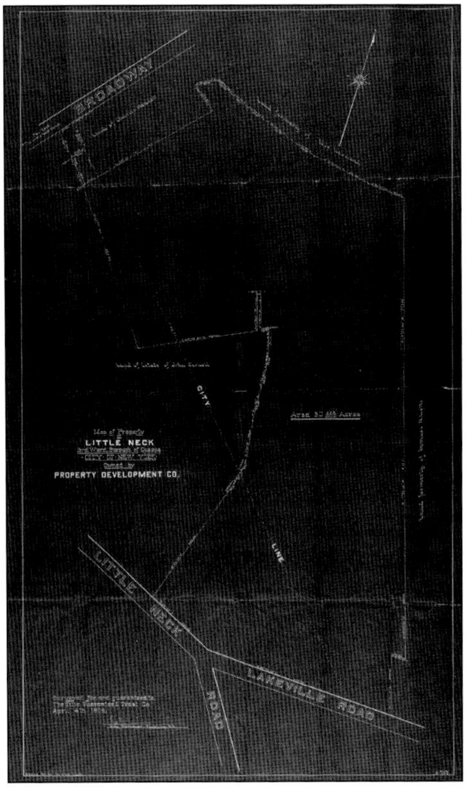

Development in 1908. As the first decade of the 20th century came to a close, more farmland was sold off for the establishment of new developments. Seen here is a rare blueprint survey map of the John Cornell property, located on the southern outskirts of Little Neck on the Nassau County line. This area would become known as the Uplands.

Little Neck Hills. It was in 1910 that Little Neck Hills was established with financing by Dwight Murray Realty Company and developed by the Little Neck Hills Development Corporation. In 1920, gas lines where introduced to that area for the first time. Approximately 13 homes in the area were furnished with gas, which was used for cooking.

Another View of the Hills. Here is another postcard view of the beautiful homes of Little Neck Hills around 1922. Homes were available for the starting price of $5,000.

Little Neck in 1909. Here is Westmoreland Avenue (now Westmoreland Street) as it appeared in the 1909 publication *Long Island To-day* by Frederick Ruther. The view of these stunning Westmoreland homes is looking south down Westmoreland Street from Fortieth Avenue. The image at bottom shows a stream of water flowing through the undeveloped woodlands of Little Neck in the Westmoreland section, which was developed on the former homestead of Benjamin Woolley.

54 LITTLE NECK AND GREAT NECK

Westmoreland Avenue, Little Neck

A Brook in the Woods near Little Neck

BAYVIEW AVENUE. This c. 1919 postcard shows the slowly developing Little Neck along Bayview Avenue. The avenue derives its name from the homestead of the DeForest family, who named their farm Bayview.

WELCOME TO BROWVALE. This 1928 image shows the entrance to yet another new development in Little Neck Hills, named Browvale. Developed by the Browvale Homes Corporation, the new subdivision featured English-style Tudor homes made of stucco, containing eight to nine rooms. The advertising billboard seen here at the intersection of Northern Boulevard and Browvale Drive (today's Browvale Lane) says it all. "Browvale Hills, Little Neck," the sign reads, "Where Nature Did Her Best!" (Percy Loomis Sperr collection.)

BROWVALE HILLS. By the 1930s, Browvale transferred development rights to the Vanzan Realty Company, which became responsible for selling these English-style stucco homes on the hill. This photograph serves as another example of Little Neck's transformation from rural country town to modern upper-middle-class enclave.

SELLING BROWVALE. Located just off Little Neck Parkway, near Browvale Drive, stood this small real estate office that offered information on buying a house in Browvale.

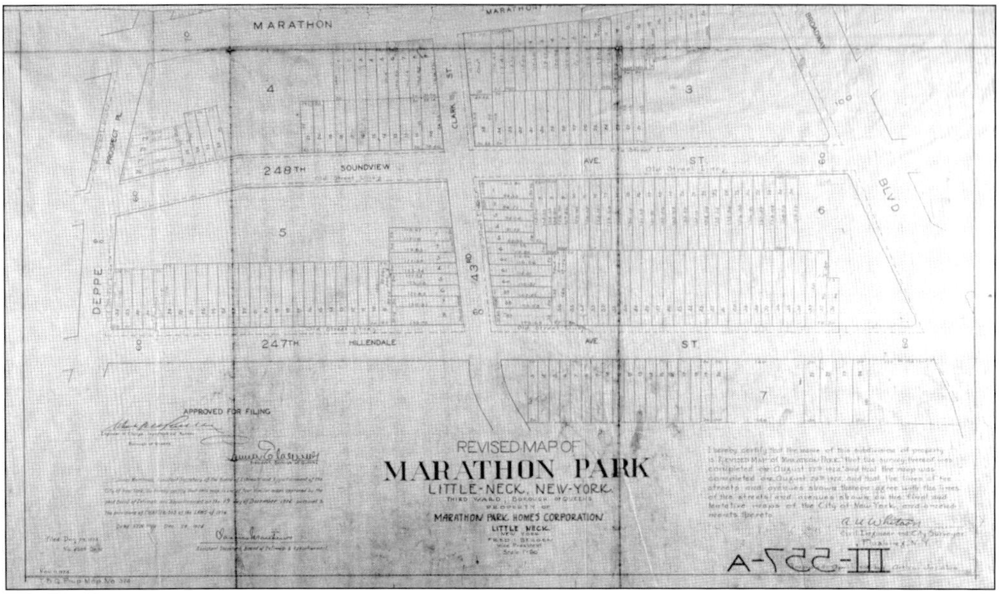

Mapping out Marathon. Marathon Park was established in the mid-1910s. Here is an overview map showing available lots in August 1924. Note how the map features the old and new street names. Queens County converted the majority of its street names between 1914 and 1919. Every neighborhood in the borough had its own set of street names, numbers, and avenues, which made for much confusion as the county became developed and rural areas became more closely linked as the population became denser. The old street names shown are Hillendale Avenue (247th Street), Soundview Avenue (248th Street), and Clarke Street (Forty-third Avenue). (Maps and Illustrations, Archives at Queens Borough Public Library.)

A View of Marathon Park. Here is a rare postcard showing an underdeveloped Marathon Park in the summer of 1915. Developed by the John M. Riehle Company and the Marathon Park Homes Corporation, the latest subdivision in Little Neck, situated north of the boulevard, boasted that it featured homes that were well heated and had modern conveniences for electric appliances with prices for homes ranging from $5,260 to $5,590. The developer promised that all homes provided "Sunlight and fresh air—Nature's great tonic." (Bob Stonehill collection.)

Van Nostrand Court. The celebrated Little Neck family of Van Nostrand lives on with the small subdivision of Van Nostrand Court. One of several private back roads in Little Neck, Van Nostrand Court is a small area tucked away along a 15-foot-wide street between Glenwood Street, West End Drive, and Pembroke Avenue. Developed by the McBride Ogden Construction Corporation, the small enclave is located on what was the William Van Nostrand farm. The subdivision began development on June 3, 1925, and the semiattached homes, built in the English garden fashion, sold very quickly. (Bob Stonehill collection.)

A Garden on the Boulevard. Seen here is Raymond Newton Hyde's Mayflower Antique Shop, which was located on the south side of Northern Boulevard just after Browvale Drive.

OLD LITTLE NECK PARKWAY. Looking south from Northern Boulevard, little Neck Parkway (then known as Little Neck Road) is depicted in 1928. Union Chapel can be seen to the right, and the cottages are seen to the left.

COMMUNITY CHURCH OF LITTLE NECK. In 1926, the Union Chapel, which was originally built in 1864 as a Methodist church on Little Neck Parkway just south of Northern Boulevard, became the Community Church of Little Neck. The building, shown here, was erected in 1950 with the formal dedication occurring on November 18, 1951. The old Union Chapel can still be seen standing on the right. Dr. Harold Pattison was the church's first minister. Bloodgood H. Cutter donated the land and was present for the laying of the cornerstone in 1864. In his book of poems, he wrote the following about the event: "To the Gospel cause I gave this ground, / To benefit the people round, / Some do the Episcopal form reject, / And some the Presbyterian neglect."

Last Days of Old Ways. This is one of the last photographs ever taken of the old Poole General Store and the Van Nostrand hotel, captured on October 7, 1926. The structures would be torn down within a year for the widening of Northern Boulevard. John Hoagland and his partner Frederick Snell originally owned the hotel, seen in the background to the right at the Little Neck Parkway intersection, in 1875. The general store in the foreground on the right was operated by Schenck and Van Nostrand and then finally the Sutphin Bros. In 1887, the Schenck General Store became the first location in Little Neck history, commercial or residential, to feature the latest wonder of the age—a telephone. They were the only Little Neck listing in the Metropolitan Telephone and Telegraph Company phone book for many years until the LIRR depot had its telephone installed in 1899.

Traffic on a Sunday Afternoon. What better way to enjoy a Sunday drive than to be stuck in traffic on the old Little Neck Road? This seemingly endless line of cars is traveling north toward the Northern Boulevard intersection; drivers are probably coming from the south shore of Long Island after a day at the beach. This photograph was taken on May 22, 1927.

LAST DAYS OF OLD LANDING HOUSE ROAD. Once Little Neck Parkway passed Northern Boulevard heading north, it became Old House Landing Road. The parkway has served as one of the town's main thoroughfares for hundreds of years, beginning as a footpath for the Native Americans who originally inhabited the area. They were members of the Algonquin Nation who referred to themselves as Matinecock, or "Place of the Hilly Country." In this view, looking north from 250th Street on March 19, 1931, one can see the homes of the Waters family homestead on the left just passed the billboards. (Edgar E. Rutter Photographs, Archives at Queens Borough Public Library.)

THE SCHNEIDER BLOCK. Built in 1914, the Schneider business block is situated on the north side of Northern Boulevard between Little Neck Parkway and Westmoreland Place. It features apartments above and retail space below. Today, it is the location of the Greek Isles Restaurant. (Bob Stonehill collection.)

A Small Wooden Church. This small wooden church, located next door to the Schneider business building, was the Baptist Church of Little Neck.

Welcome to Little Neck, 1930. Looking east on Northern Boulevard from 249th Street, this January 1930 photograph depicts Little Neck at the start of the Great Depression. The sign on the left, issued by the chamber of commerce, reads, "Now you are in Little Neck! Make your choice of a fine location."

VAN NOSTRAND HOMESTEAD. Once the building boom of the mid-1920s came to Little Neck, some homes had to be sacrificed while others were saved and physically moved to another location. Such was the fate for the Van Nostrand homestead, known as the Old Oaks, which was moved from its spot on Northern Boulevard to make way for the new movie theater. Originally owned by David L. Van Nostrand, the home was occupied later by his brother William H. Van Nostrand, who lived there with his family until the home was moved in 1929. The name of the property originates with the home's original owner, Capt. Valentine Peters, who named it after the huge oak trees that surrounded the property. Today, the home stands at the northwest corner of Pembroke Avenue and Westmoreland Place.

THE LITTLE THEATER BEAUTIFUL. The Little Neck Theater was built on the site of the Van Nostrand family homestead in 1929. Paul Raisler and Ruth Wright operated the theater privately until 1941. It was sold to the Interior Circuit of theaters but then back to private ownership in 1952 to Charles Friedman, a resident of Great Neck. The Little Neck Theater opened on January 18, 1929, with Jack Holt in *Submarine*. The theater remained in operation until the mid-1980s. (NYC Municipal Archives, Tax Photos Unit.)

Little Neck Theater Program. The Little Neck theater was known as "the Little Theatre Beautiful." Patrons of the theater would receive this program of the wonderful films that would be playing; it featured photograph stills from the movies along with small synopses and the show times. Playing during the weekend of June 20–22, 1935, was *Mississippi*, starring Bing Crosby, W.C. Fields, and Joan Bennet. Then, from June 23–25, moviegoers could watch *Reckless* with Jean Harlow and William Powell.

LITTLE NECK

NORTHERN BOULEVARD, LITTLE NECK, L. I.
"THE LITTLE THEATRE BEAUTIFUL"

THURSDAY - FRIDAY - SATURDAY — JUNE 20 - 21 - 22

Roll down the river—on the most colorful showboat of all —with

BING CROSBY

crooning new tunes

— with —

W. C. FIELDS

and

JOAN BENNETT

— in —

"MISSISSIPPI"

also RICHARD BARTHELMESS in "4 HOURS TO KILL"

SUNDAY - MONDAY - TUESDAY — JUNE 23 - 24 - 25

Glorious with music! Bulging with fun! M-G-M-'s mighty melody-drama masterpiece! Cruise on "The Honeymoon Ship!" Peep at the "Neon Pajama Parade!" Tango "'Neath a Peruvian Moon!" It's bigger than a $6.60 Broadway show!

Jean Harlow

and

William Powell

— in —

"RECKLESS"

— with —

Franchot Tone

also "HOLD 'EM YALE" with BUSTER CRABBE

MARCUS SISKIND
Optometrist
PHONE BAYSIDE 9-6780
LITTLE NECK THEA. BLDG

Telephone: Manhasset 1334
"Call 'Round Any Old Time" at
CHARLIE SCHMIDT'S TAVERN
and be entertained by GEORGE E. KRAUSE
World Famous One-Handed Pianist
118 Plandome Road — Manhasset, L. I.
200 feet off Northern Boulevard
The Finest Bar—Serving the Finest Liquors — Good Food

Tel.: BAyside 9-1491 — LITTLE NECK'S LARGEST RETAIL FRUIT MARKET
HIGH GRADE FRUITS & VEGETABLES
NEW NORTH SHORE FRUIT EXCHANGE
254-15 NORTHERN BLVD., Opp. Little Neck Theatre
• ORDERS DELIVERED •
Clubs, Restaurants and Fruit Stores Supplied at Wholesale Prices

SCREENS — SCREEN DOORS
BERDICK LUMBER & TRIM CO.
221-18 MERRICK ROAD
LAURELTON
Phone: LAurelton 8-1400
Garage Doors — Sheet Rock — Mill Work

Buy Screens and Weatherstrips Direct From a Manufacturer
ROYAL WEATHERSTRIP & SCREEN CO.
221-20 Merrick Rd., Laurelton
Phone: LAurelton 8-1400
Screens — Weatherstrips — Caulking

famous — **SUKI YAKI** — dinner $1.00
NIPPON INN
LITTLE NECK PARKWAY, near Nassau Blvd., LITTLE NECK, N. Y.
Yes: We Do Catering for any occasion — Real ORIENTAL Dishes — Tel.: BAyside 9-3461

PANCHARD
near Jones' Beach, Massapequa
on the Merrick Road
DINING - DANCING - NIGHTLY
Continental Dinners $1.00 up
Wines and Liquors
No Cover Charge

FOR PROTECTION—Drive in
STANDARD SUPER-SERVICE STATION
259th St. and Northern Blvd.
Great Neck, L. I.
Gas - Oil - Batteries - Tubes
Car Washing - Greasing
Guaranteed Car Waxing

FOR ADVERTISING RATES IN THIS PROGRAM inquire
AMBASSADOR STUDIOS, Inc.
191-18 JAMAICA AVE., HOLLIS, L. I. — Tel.: HOllis 5-4090

LUDWIG SCHOLTZ
We Call and Deliver
Fine Antiques and Furniture
General Repairing and Refinishing
Hand Caning — Rush Seating to Order
Alcohol Mark Proof Finishing Done
Furniture you have often repaired, never satisfied, let me try them.
252-24 Northern Blvd. — Little Neck
Tel.: BAyside 9-4035

NEW HYDE PARK PUBLIC GOLF CLUB, Inc.
Lakeville Rd., New Hyde Park, L. I.
Tel.: Floral Park 2467
18 HOLES
RATES— WEEK DAYS - - - - $1.00
SATURDAYS - - - - 1.50
SUN. & HOLIDAYS - - 2.00
NICHOLAS FABRIZIO, Mgr.

Sea Food — **MIDTOWN CAFE'** — Steaks
253-32 NORTHERN BLVD., LITTLE NECK
Entrance also to Dining and Cocktail Rooms around the corner
Serving the finest BEER - WINES - LIQUORS
Visit our Beautiful Rainbow and Silver Rooms, something different
Luncheon . . . 35c — . . . Sandwiches . . . — Dinner . . . 65c

Things to Do, Places to See. On the reverse of the program was a listing of places to eat and have fun after seeing a movie. After seeing *Mississippi* or *Reckless*, patrons could continue their fun over at Charlie Schmidt's tavern on Plandome Road, located just off Northern Boulevard in neighboring Great Neck. George E. Krause, who was billed as "the World Famous One Handed Pianist," entertained guests at the tavern. Or if one was in the mood for something more low-key, there was the Nippon Inn on Little Neck Parkway, near Nassau Boulevard (the LIE). There, patrons could enjoy its famous Suki Yaki dinner for a dollar.

CONTINUOUS PERFORMANCE
DAILY FROM 1:30 to 11 P. M.
Doors Open at 1:00 P. M.
Program Subject to Change at Discretion of Management

LITTLE NECK THEATRE

"Little Theatre Beautiful" — "Where The Voice Is Human"
"A United Long Island Theatre"
Northern Boulevard, Little Neck, L. I. PAUL RAISLER, Mgr.
Phone: Great Neck 222 and Bayside 9-6471

Monday to Saturday
Matinee: Children 15c; Adults 20c
Evenings, Sundays and Holidays
Children 20c; Adults 35c

SMOKING NOW PERMITTED IN THE ENTIRE RIGHT HAND SIDE OF THEATRE

SUN. and MON. JUNE 16 and 17
DOUBLE FEATURE
"Unwelcome Stranger"
— with —
JACK HOLT - MONA BARRIE
— also —
"CASINO MURDER CASE"
— with —
PAUL LUKAS - ALISON SKIPWORTH
Selected Short Subjects

TUES. and WED. JUNE 18 and 19
"THE MYSTERY OF EDWIN DROOD"
— with —
CLAUDE RAINS
Selected Short Subjects
WED.—BANK NITE—If you have not already registered, do so now. No charge for registration.

THURS., FRI., SAT. JUNE 20, 21, 22
DOUBLE FEATURE
"MISSISSIPPI"
— with —
BING CROSBY - W. C. FIELDS
— also —
Richard Barthelmess
— in —
"FOUR HOURS TO KILL"
Selected Short Subjects

SUN., MON., TUES. JUNE 23, 24, 25
DOUBLE FEATURE
JEAN HARLOW WILLIAM POWELL
— in —
"RECKLESS"
— also —
"HOLD 'EM YALE"
— with —
PATRICIA ELLIS - BUSTER CRABBE
Selected Short Subjects

WED. and THURS. JUNE 26 and 27
"VANESSA"
— with —
HELEN HAYES
ROBERT MONTGOMERY
Selected Short Subjects
WED.—BANK NITE—If you have not already registered, do so now. No charge for registration.

FRI. and SAT. JUNE 28 and 29
DOUBLE FEATURE
Edward Everett Horton
Karen Morley
— in —
"TEN DOLLAR RAISE"
— also —
"PRINCESS O'HARA"
— with —
CHESTER MORRIS - JEAN PARKER
Selected Short Subjects

SUN. and MON. JUNE 30 and JULY 1
DOUBLE FEATURE
By Popular Request
The 3 Prize Academy of Arts Photoplay
IT HAPPENED ONE NIGHT
— with —
CLAUDETTE COLBERT
CLARK GABLE
— also —
"THE SCOUNDREL"
— with —
NOEL COWARD - JULIE HAYDON
Selected Short Subjects

TUES. and WED. JULY 2 and 3
"PRIVATE WORLDS"
— with —
CLAUDETTE COLBERT
CHARLES BOYER
Selected Short Subjects
WED.—BANK NITE—If you have not already registered, do so now. No charge for registration.

THURS., FRI., SAT. JULY 4, 5, 6
GEORGE ARLISS
— in —
"CARDINAL RICHELIEU"
— Matinees Only —
BUCK JONES
in "BORDER BRIGANDS"
Selected Short Subjects

SUN., MON. and TUES. JULY 7, 8 and 9
DOUBLE FEATURE
Paul Muni - Karen Morley
— in —
"BLACK FURY"
— also —
"LOVE IN BLOOM"
— with —
DIXIE LEE - BURNS & ALLEN
Selected Short Subjects

WED. and THURS. JULY 10 and 11
"DEVIL IS A WOMAN"
— with —
MARLENE DIETRICH
Selected Short Subjects
WED.—BANK NITE—If you have not already registered, do so now. No charge for registration.

FRI. and SAT. JULY 12 and 13
DOUBLE FEATURE
"IT'S A SMALL WORLD"
— with —
SPENCER TRACY - WENDY BARRIE
— also —
"FLORENTINE DAGGER"
— with —
DONALD WOODS
MARGARET LINDSAY
Selected Short Subjects

AN ENTERTAINING LINEUP. The inside of the same program shows the various entertaining films and double billings that were shown at the Little Neck Theater. From Monday to Saturday, children were admitted for 15¢ and adults 20¢. On Sundays and holidays, children got in for 20¢ and adults 35¢. The theater was opened from 1:30 p.m. until 11:00 p.m. everyday.

CHRISTMAS AT THE MOVIES. If a person were living in Little Neck during the Christmas week of 1940, he or she could see the following great films: *Knute Rockne, All American*, starring Pat O'Brien, Gale Page, and Ronald Reagan; *No Time for Comedy*, starring James Stewart and Rosalind Russell; and *The Howards of Virginia* with Cary Grant and Martha Scott.

Cinematic Stocking Stuffers. Here is the holiday feature film lineup for Christmas week 1940. Note all the faces of Hollywood's biggest stars peeking out from Christmas stockings.

Queens Library Little Neck–Douglaston Branch. The first library in the area began as a traveling library located inside of Public School No. 94 in 1915. The library was overseen by the school's principal Anna Brett and was founded by the Mothers Club of Little Neck. With the help of the Little Neck Civic League and the Mothers Club, the two petitioned the Queens Borough Public Library to establish a brick-and-mortar location. On July 8, 1930, that dream became a reality when the branch officially opened at 248–04 Northern Boulevard. It was located here until 1962, when it moved to 251–05 Northern Boulevard in the former Bohack Supermarket. (Queens Borough Public Library Photographs, Archives at Queens Borough Pubic Library.)

A NEW POST OFFICE. The days of the independent post offices located in Buhrman's general store in the Alley and Schenck's general store ended on January 16, 1913, when an official US Post Office was established in Little Neck. A few weeks later, on February 1, two letter carriers, John Kimmons and Harry Holman, were assigned horse-drawn wagons to deliver mail in Douglaston and Little Neck. This group photograph of the branch's letter carriers is from 1931. (Robert Trombley collection.)

THE BUMBLEBEES NEST, 1930. The Bumblebees Nest Hotel was located in the southernmost extreme of Little Neck. The hotel, owned by Charles Kenniger, stood toward the end of Douglaston Parkway, a little bit south of today's Seventieth Avenue. The Vanderbilt Motor Parkway would pass less than 100 feet from the hotel, which accommodated guests and patrons who came here to drink and eat during the Vanderbilt Cup races. (Percy Loomis Sperr collection.)

WESTMORELAND GARDEN HOMES. "A Kingdom all your own," reads the real estate brochure for these garden apartments, developed by William I. Hohauser. A builder of affordable housing in the city, Hohauser built this community, Westmoreland Gardens, in 1941. Located at Little Neck Parkway and Fortieth Avenue, the garden apartments were leased for a monthly rent of $58.50. These apartments catered to the growing middle class and, a few years later, to soldiers returning from World War II.

FINE LIVING AND GOOD LEISURE. The sales pamphlet for Westmoreland Gardens advertised fun at Jones Beach, golfing at Douglaston Park, and even a local bridle path for horseback riding.

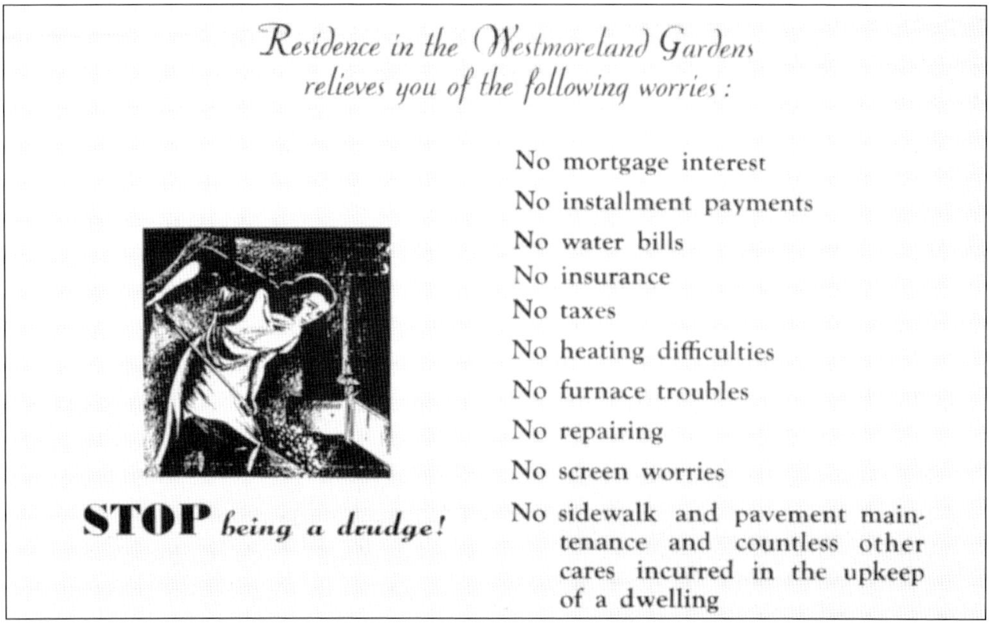

A Good Deal. The developer sold the idea of living in Westmoreland by promising the following perks: no mortgage interest, no water bills, no taxes, no repairing, and no sidewalk maintenance fees.

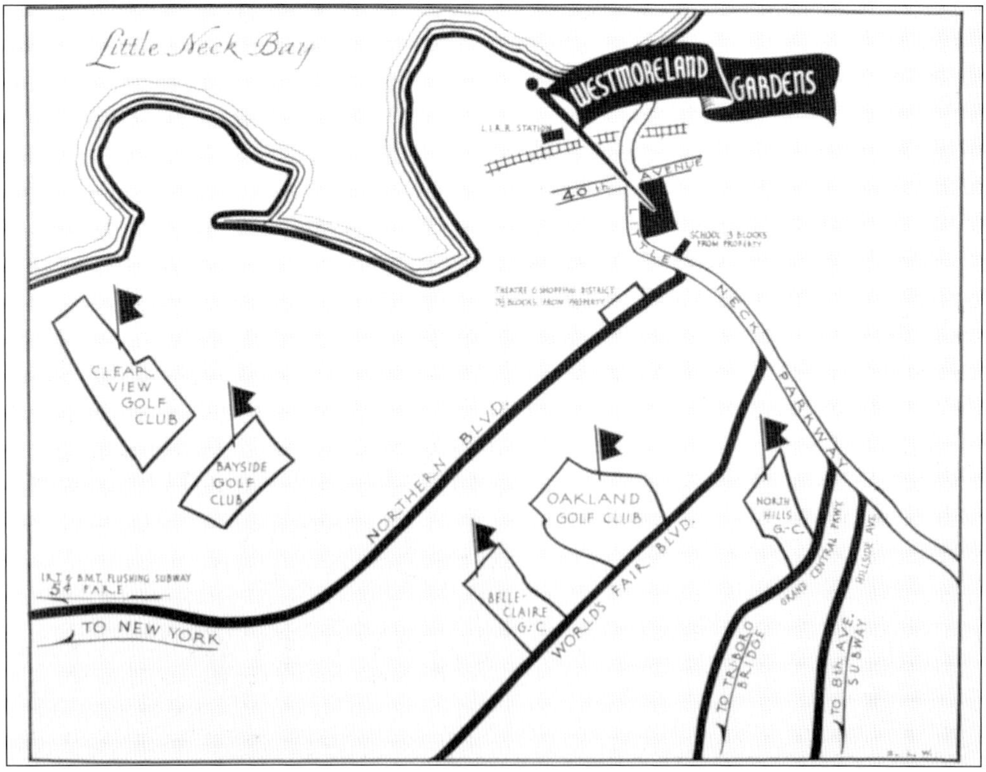

Let's Go Golfing. The map on the rear of the brochure displayed all the golf courses in the area, including the Clearview Golf Club, Bayside Golf Club, Belle-Claire Golf Club, Oakland Golf Club, and the North Hills Golf Club.

LIFE BEGINS AT WESTMORELAND GARDENS. The garden apartments offered residents open spaces and convenient access to the city via the LIRR—only 24 minutes to Manhattan with 70 trains daily. One of the other major selling points, although debatable, was "never a traffic jam over New York State's finest highways to many of Americas greatest recreation resorts."

DEEPDALE GARDENS. Named after the estate of William Kissam Vanderbilt, it was the largest federally sponsored housing cooperative built in the United States; it was designed as affordable housing for World War II and Korean War veterans.

A Beautiful Layout. Deepdale Gardens, built in 1952, is situated on 60 acres of land and is comprised of 69 buildings, containing 1,396 garden-style apartments.

PS 94. Public School 94, named after Civil War admiral David D. Porter, was built in 1915. Anna Brett was the school's first principal.

At the Border. One of the advantages of living in Little Neck is the immediate access to Long Island, for it is situated right at the border line between New York City and Nassau County. Looking west down Horace Harding Boulevard, this November 22, 1938, photograph shows the Little Neck/Great Neck border. It is through this exact path that the Long Island Expressway would be built 20 years later. Horace Harding Boulevard would be designated an expressway and serve as both an eastbound and westbound service road.

"A Good Place To Meet, A Better Place To Eat." Here is a menu for the 20th Century Diner, located on the northwest corner of Northern Boulevard and Little Neck Parkway. Built in 1935, it was operated by Charles Frishman in an old train car, and it stood until 1961, when it was torn down to build the Scobee Grill, which opened in 1962 and evolved into the Scobee Diner. The beloved diner would cease operations in 2010 and was torn down shortly after.

Protest at Scobee and Northern Boulevard. Angry citizens of Little Neck took to the streets in 1970 to protest the speeding problem on Northern Boulevard. The protestors demanded that the City of New York do something to curb vehicular speeding in the area. The old Scobee Diner can be seen on the right.

Bank of Manhattan Company. Opening on April 30, 1929, the Bank of the Manhattan Company first operated in this Federal-style building on the southwest corner of Northern Boulevard. The building was constructed on the site of Edgar C. Poole's general store, which had been torn down two years earlier. In 1955, the bank became Chase Manhattan Bank after the merger of the Bank of Manhattan Company and the Chase National Bank. Paul B. LaVelle, a chief designer for Stanford White, designed the building. For the interior of the bank, LaVelle imported black-and-green marble from Switzerland and yellow marble from France. The woodwork was done in American walnut. An American bald eagle relief is still perched above the main doorway on the bank's limestone exterior.

Little Neck–Douglaston Ambulance Service. The Little Neck–Douglaston Community Ambulance Corps began in Douglaston in 1958. In the first month of its existence, the ambulance corps started a house-to-house canvass for funds with a goal of $15,000. Operations began on March 30, 1958, with 34 attendants qualified in first aid. Twenty-four hours after service began, the corps got its first call and took a heart victim to North Shore Hospital. The Lions Club contributed $500 to purchase equipment. Donated by the Bayside Volunteer Ambulance Corps on January 12, 1958, the first ambulance was a secondhand 1947 Buick. The ground-breaking ceremony for the future home of the Little Neck–Douglaston Community Ambulance Corps took place in September 1961. The original building had two separate garage doors leading into the ambulance garages on the first floor. On the second floor was a large meeting room/crew lounge. In 1981, the building underwent a $50,000 renovation. (Little Neck–Douglaston Ambulance Service.)

Temple Torah. One of many synagogues in Little Neck and Douglaston, Temple Torah was built on part of the old Cornell homestead and has been serving the Jewish community of eastern Queens since its creation in 1957.

Eight

MATINECOCK

CHIEF WILD PIGEON. The peoples of the Algonquin Nation called the land upon which they reigned Matinecock, which translates to "People of the Hilly County" or "the Hunting Place." This truly was the case for these Lenni-Lenape–speaking people who hunted for fish or clams in the Little Neck Bay, which was overlooked by a landscape covered with beautifully green tree-topped rolling hills. Seen here is Chief Wild Pigeon, the great-great-uncle of Donna Barron (the author of this book's foreword) of the Barron and Waters families of Little Neck. Born in Little Neck in 1873, James Edwards Waters, known as Chief Wild Pigeon, was elected grand sachem of the Montauk tribe after the death of his father, John M. Waters. Waters was chief of the Matinecock and Montaukett reservations. He was a member of the Flushing Historical Society (now the Queens Historical Society) and had been employed at the general post office in Manhattan. Chief Wild Pigeon led the charge against the City of New York in the late 1920s when it decided to widen Northern Boulevard, thus eliminating the family cemetery. (Donna Barron collection.)

The John M. Waters Homestead. This rare c. 1890s photograph from the private collection of Donna Barron shows the homestead of John M. Waters, which was located on the northwest corner of Northern Boulevard and Little Neck Parkway, the former site of the Scobee diner. (Donna Barron collection.)

Madie Heather Flower Waters. Here is a beautiful photograph of Madie Heather Flower Waters, the great-great-aunt of Donna Barron. (Donna Barron collection.)

Installing a New Chief. In 1958, John Standing Waters was installed as chief of the Matinecock. Here is a rare photograph of the installation ceremony that was held at Zion Church. His daughter Maddie Heather Flower Waters stands to his left. It was 300 years earlier when Chief Tackapausha disputed land claims against Thomas Hicks and Richard Cornell. Hicks would later lead a militant mob and drive the Matinecock off their land. The event would be known infamously as the Battle of Madnan's Neck. They still forged on, as seen here, more than three centuries later. Chief Tackapausha was the great chief of the Matinecock, the son of Agagonmon, known as "One-Eye," the grand sachem of lower New York state. (Both, Donna Barron collection.)

Old House Landing Road. For more than a century, the head of Little Neck Parkway was known as Old House Landing Road. It was here that Jacob Treadwell (the great-great-great-grandfather of Donna Barron) first settled when it was known as Gabler's Creek in 1853 on a 1.5-acre property, surrounded by stately poplars and maples trees. The former boatyard seen here was the hub of a huge oyster industry, which existed from 1860 until 1900. It was people like Treadwell and Capt. Christian William Kirkman who helped cultivate this industry that provided the renowned Little Neck clams. In the 1860s, Kirkman planted oyster seeds, and Little Neck Bay turned into a spawning ground. In its heyday, the site on Old House Landing Road saw as many as 70 men working Little Neck Bay; they were able to make $18 to $20 weekly, which is between $500 and $600 in today's money.

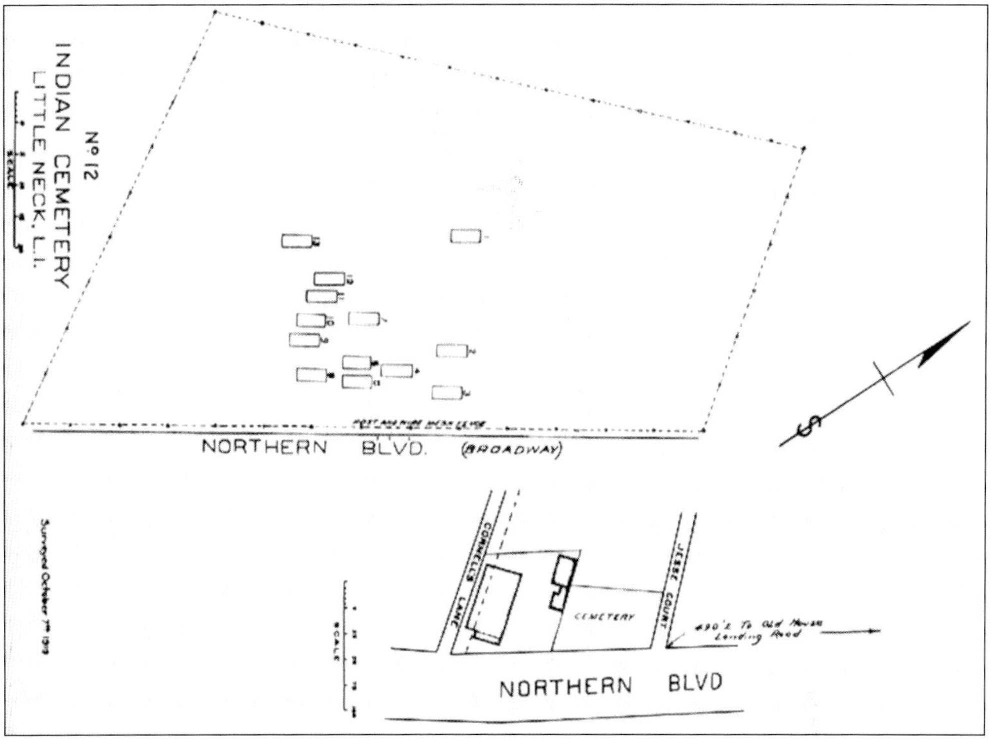

Mapping out the Indian Cemetery. Surveyed by the Queens Topographical Bureau on October 7, 1919, and published in the bureau's 1931 report *Description of Private and Family Cemeteries in the Borough of Queens,* the Waters cemetery stood on the north side of Northern Boulevard between Cornell Lane and Jessie Court for 200 years. In the late 1920s, the cemetery became targeted for elimination when the city decided to widen Northern Boulevard as part of its citywide road and highway development initiative. The city identified 13 gravestone markers. Six were not readable but seven were. The interred included those of husband and wife, Charles (1826–1896) and Jane Waters (1831–1901); their children Sabra Eva (1861–1890), James, who died at eight months old in 1859, and son Joel Stephen, who died at three years and three months old in 1859; and James W. Smith (1892–1904), the only son of David and Fannie Smith.

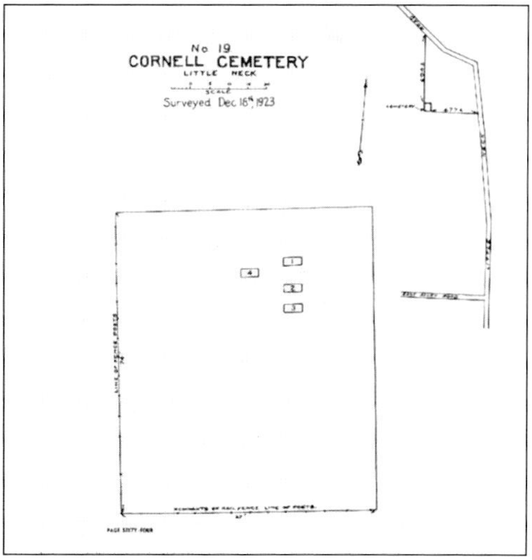

Cornell Cemetery Survey. The Queens Topographical Bureau surveyed the Cornell cemetery on December 18, 1923. There were four graves marked. The cemetery was located at the northeast corner of Little Neck Parkway and Horace Harding Boulevard at the bottom of a hill upon which stood the Cornell homestead. Also buried here were Emeline Penny, who died in 1850 at 31; John Cornell, who died in 1847 at 75; and Atletter Ann, daughter of Charles and Ann Herrick, who died in 1849 at only 6. The Cornell family lived in Little Neck for five generations. They were descended from Richard Cornell, a Quaker who had come to Flushing from Rhode Island in 1643 after obtaining a land grant from the Dutch West India Company.

Cornell Cemetery. Photographed on April 1927 by the Queens Topographical Bureau is the grave of Samuel Cornell, who departed this life on December 28, 1841, at 20 years and 11 months old. Note the grave's epitaph, "Strangers, remember, you must die." The Cornell and Hicks families feuded with the Waters family for years over land. In 1905, Charles Cornell, a descendant of an early English settler, claimed the right of purchase to the Waters homestead after it lay vacant for almost five years. Against the wishes of the Waters family, Cornell built six homes on the large unsurveyed property and ran a paved road directly through part of the old Indian cemetery. The Waters family tried to stop him but lost the battle in court. Without a marker or a sign, the remains of many Native American ancestors still lay under the ironically named Cornell Lane. (Office of the Queens Borough President, Topographical Bureau.)

Matinecock Burial Ground. Overgrowth covers the graves of the Waters cemetery as it endures its final days in this 1929 photograph. Within two years, it would be removed in one of the biggest and most tragic news stories of the day to occur in Little Neck. (Percy Loomis Sperr collection.)

Excavating the Cemetery. In one of the saddest photographs ever taken by the Queens Topographical Bureau, the excavation of the Waters family cemetery occurred on October 20, 1931. Three members of the Waters family stand huddled together as residents of Little Neck look on curiously from behind the chicken wire fence. Very little privacy was afforded the family as the remains were placed in pine box coffins and stacked to the side. Those interred in this cemetery were buried in the European fashion—that is with a stone marker bearing the name of the deceased and displaying their date of birth and passing. Some burials discovered within the city limits had the remains of the departed covered in oyster shells. In others instances, certain tribes would bury their loved ones vertically. (Office of the Queens Borough President, Topographical Bureau.)

Digging up the Past. The layer-by-layer excavation of the cemetery continues. During the two-week-long digging project, Queens Borough president George Upton Harvey invited George Gustave Heye of the Museum of the American Indian, Heye Foundation, located at 1 Bowling Green in Manhattan, to attend the exhumation and to help recover Indian artifacts. This went strictly against a court-ordered mandate from the Queens County Civil Court stating that no artifacts were to be removed, and if that if any are unearthed, they are to be turned over to members of the family. This was not done, and it would take almost nine decades for the remains taken from the site to be returned to the family. (Office of the Queens Borough President, Topographical Bureau.)

WIDENING NORTHERN BOULEVARD. This October 7, 1926, photograph was taken looking east on Northern Boulevard toward Marathon Parkway. The old volunteer firehouse can be seen on the left as more land is cleared for the first stage of development and widening of the boulevard.

MAKING ROOM FOR PROGRESS. Here, the old estates and wooded areas along Northern Boulevard are cleared for the widening of the boulevard as more eastbound and westbound lanes are created due to the advent of the automobile and the accelerated development of new communities in Little Neck and Nassau County.

Burial Site at Zion Church. In another painful chapter, one that offered some closure but little consolation, the remains taken from the site on Northern Boulevard were reinterred at Zion Cemetery in a mass grave, which was adorned with a large granite boulder with the following inscription: "Here Rest the Last of the Matinecoc Indians." The memorial was later adopted by the Maj. Thomas Wickes Chapter of the Daughters of the American Revolution in 1948.

Coming Full Circle. In 2017, Chief Harry Wallace of the Unkechaug Nation of Long Island, Matinecock chief Osceola Townsend, and Matinecock Turkey Clan chief Reggie Ceasar joined the Matinecock Nation at a special burial ceremony at Zion Episcopal Church to mark the long-awaited homecoming of Matinecock remains. The skeletal remains were located at the Museum of Arts and Sciences in Florida. Working with the Native American Graves Protection and Repatriation Act Review Committee of the Florida Department of State, Chief Wallace, an attorney, was able to prove that these remains were taken from the excavation of the Waters family's private burial ground during the widening of Northern Boulevard in 1931. The spirits of the family's past have come full circle back to their homeland.

MATINECOCK WAY. In September 2015, with help of the Bayside Historical Society and the author, the intersection of Northern Boulevard and Marathon Parkway was renamed Matinecock Way. The intersection is where the Matinecock fought their last stand against Thomas Hicks. The land grab is the only recorded incident of such activity in Flushing Township history. (Bayside Historical Society.)

A LAST GLIMPSE. As this brief history of Douglaston and Little Neck concludes, let us celebrate the efforts of the many civic-minded individuals who have worked so hard to preserve the architectural and natural beauty and epic history of these two beloved neighborhoods. Their dedication has resulted in the successful preservation of the area's legacy and has allowed for both towns to remain great for many generations to come. Seen here is a rare image of the annual Douglaston-Little Neck Parade taken more than 50 years ago. The parade first began in 1927 as a tribute to the legacy of a great American town. (Donna Barron collection.)

Bibliography

Allaback, Sarah. *The First American Women Architects*. Champaign, IL: University of Illinois Press, 2008.

Barron, Donna. *The Life & Customs of My People from the Days Gone By: The Long Island Indians of the North Shore: Little Neck, New York*. Seattle, WA: CreateSpace, 2014.

bklyn.newspapers.com

Brown, Henry Collins. *From Alley Pond to Rockefeller Center*. New York, NY: E.P. Dutton, 1936.

Brown, Joseph H. and Dr. Arthur Mallon. *Bayside in Colonial Times*. Bayside, NY: Bayside Historical Society, 1989.

douglashistory.co.uk

Fowler, George C., and Ernestine H. Fowler. *Through the Years in Little Neck & Douglaston*. New York, NY: self-published, 1963.

Gubernick, Loys. *Little Neck Then & Now*. Bayside, NY: Published Ink-it Printing, 1987.

Little Neck Community Association. *The History of Little Neck*. Little Neck, NY: self-published, 1952.

Pelham Bolton, Reginald. *Indian Life of Long Ago in the City of New York*. New York, NY: Harmony Books, 1972.

Riley, Rev. Lester Leake. *The Chronicle of Little Neck and Douglaston, Long Island: Part of the Little Neck–Douglaston Division of the Long Island Tercentenary Commemoration of Queens*. Little Neck, NY: Long Island Tercentenary Committee of Queens, 1936.

Seyfried, Vincent F. *The Long Island Rail Road: A Comprehensive History, Part Two: The Flushing, North Shore & Central Railroad*. Garden City, NY: self-published, 1963.

———. *Flushing in the Civil War Era: 1837–1865*. Garden City, NY: Queens Community Series, 2001.

———. *New York and North Shore Traction Company*. Garden City, NY: self-published, 1955.

Turner Richardson, Catherine. *Little Madnans Neck and the Alley: A Brief History of Douglaston. LI*. Douglaston, NY: self-published, 1947.

Wolfe, Kevin. *This Salubrious Spot: The First 100 Years at Douglas Manor 1906–2006*. Douglaston, NY: The Douglas Manor Association, 2006.

Zion Episcopal Church. *Sesquicentennial, 1830–1980*. Douglaston, NY: Zion Episcopal Church, 1980.

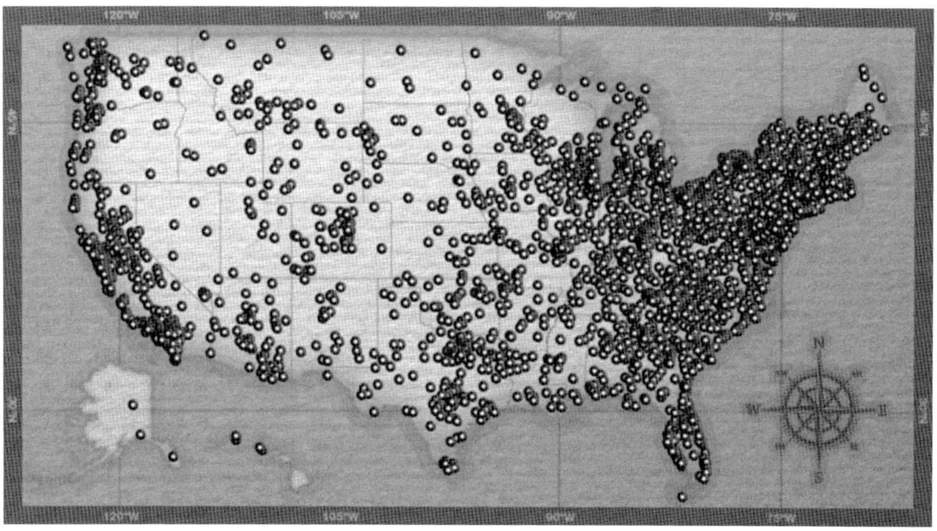